Gaining Ground as a
TRULY Evangelistic Church

www.GoodSoil.com

Good Soil
Evangelism & Discipleship

Published by
Good Soil Evangelism and Discipleship

ISBN: 978-1-951672-12-6

Library of Congress Cataloging-in-Publications Data (application pending)

Printed in USA.

Gaining Ground as a TRULY Evangelistic Church

Cover Design and Artwork: Tetra Design Co
Interior Design: Tetra Design Co
Custom Photography: Chelsea Foster, Tetra Design Co
Stock Photography: 123rf.com

Authors: Haston, Wayne (1947–), Levy, David (1966–),
Southwell, Randy (1971–), Thomas, Gilbert H. (1959–)

Email: Info@GoodSoil.com
Web: www.GoodSoil.com
Order: 1.877.959.2293

Authors

Wayne Haston, PhD, served on local church pastoral staffs for 29 years. During those years, he was a seminary professor—teaching seminarians to apply in church ministry what they were learning in seminary classes. In 1995, he joined the staff of ABWE – Association of Baptists for World Evangelism and trained missionaries and international church leaders around the world. With the assistance of some ABWE colleagues, Wayne developed Good Soil Evangelism and Discipleship in 2007 to equip believers for worldview-relevant evangelism and discipleship.

David Levy, MDiv, is a first-generation Christian. Raised Jewish, he came to faith in Christ as a high school senior. He served in pastoral ministry for 24 years. As a senior pastor, David attended a Good Soil Evangelism and Discipleship Seminar. He embraced the Good Soil philosophy, used Good Soil resources, and saw God use them to bring adults to Christ, follow in believer's baptism, and join their church. In 2019, the Lord directed David to join the Good Soil team at ABWE. He is excited to come alongside pastors and churches to encourage them to fulfill the great commission locally with a global impact.

A third-generation missionary, **Randy Southwell, MDiv,** grew up in the country of Portugal. He served for 18 years as a church planter in south Brazil. While there, he was introduced to Good Soil Evangelism & Discipleship, used the principles and resources in his ministry, and began to help train others around Brazil. Now he enjoys teaching and training around the world.

After 23 years of serving in Portugal as a church planter, 14 of those years as the Team Leader, **Gilbert Thomas, DMin,** brought his experience in working with teams and training missionaries to Good Soil Evangelism and Discipleship in 2008. For years Gil has used chronological Bible teaching as his principal form of evangelism and has discipled and trained missionaries all over Western Europe. Now he enjoys telling the story as well.

Foreword

Thank you for picking up a copy of this book. As stated on the cover, this is a "collaborative book" from your friends at Good Soil Evangelism & Discipleship. We have had the joy of seeing thousands of people in the United States and around the world take Good Soil training and use our resources. We are encouraged that God is drawing many people to Himself and using these tools to help people make disciples.

One thing we have noticed many times, however, is that attending the training can be like a camp experience. People learn a lot, make commitments, and leave the training excited to do more to make disciples. But sometimes they go no further. Pastors and leaders go home, put the books on the shelf, and do nothing more with them. Or they just don't know where to start to help their church become more evangelistic.

This book seeks to address that dilemma by providing a pathway for those who really want to see things change. It shares tangible, attainable steps and how to take them.

So, in the first section of the book, we start with a pastor who is struggling with just that problem: neither he nor his church is reaching out. (That is happening more than any of us would like to admit.) Read about his struggle and what he and his friends do to begin to solve his predicament. The story is a parable founded on real events and struggles from our lives and derived from our nearly 150 years of missionary and pastoral experience.

The second section of the book is comprised of short chapters revealing what we have found over years of ministry to be essentials of a TRULY evangelistic church. We have built those essentials into a helpful model. At the end of each chapter are questions to reflect and act upon what you have learned. Please take the time to interact and work through these. There is also a leader's guide available to help you work through these essentials with a team. Personal illustrations in this part of the book come from Wayne's 40 years of pastoral and training experience.

Enjoy the book! And please feel free to contact us with any questions you may have or let us know how the book has helped you.

The Good Soil Team

The Story

Frustrated!

Brandon Austin couldn't remember a time in his life when he was more frustrated, and he couldn't figure out why. Three years ago, he had moved to his third pastorate since graduating from seminary, serving as a youth pastor for 18 months in northern Pennsylvania, and then serving for 42 months as the pastor of a small church just over the PA/NY border. His new church was consistently running just over 200 every Sunday and had not dropped in attendance since he had come. Sure, he knew it had not grown in attendance either, but even after the honeymoon period, attendance was solid. Brandon was the senior pastor in this upstate New York church with a youth pastor and full-time secretary on staff with him.

His people loved him, his wife Rebekah, and their four children, too. Having church members to their house for dinner at least once a month seemed to be paying off. The relationships with his flock were encouraging, and they seemed eager to follow his leading. This was it. Brandon was convinced this was the church in which he would stay and invest his life. And yet, there was that gnawing frustration that wouldn't go away.

As Brandon passed the "Welcome to Pennsylvania—Pursue Your Happiness" sign, he startled himself by saying out loud, "Hmph. My happiness?" He decided to continue talking out loud, this time to God. "Lord, what is it? You know I want to serve you faithfully, to invest my life to minister for You effectively. My happiness isn't the issue. But why am I feeling so frustrated? What is wrong? Is there something I'm not admitting to myself? Help me, Lord. Show me what I need to do."

Deep down inside he suspected he knew what the problem might be. Maybe he just did not want to acknowledge it.

Special Friends

"Hey, Smitty! How's it going?" Brandon yelled out the window as he turned into the driveway. Brandon had made the three-and-a-half hour trip down to Erie, Pennsylvania, where his friends from college days had agreed to meet this year. Believe it or not, three of the four classmates who had grown so close during their college days had not missed getting together for a few days each summer for 11 years now. "Smitty," Jedediah Smith, had arranged through Airbnb for them to stay in a house near Presque Isle. The site had called it an "Erie-sistible Home."

The foursome had decided to meet in Erie this year because it seemed to be centrally located. With Brandon in upstate New York, Smitty starting a church in Huntington, West Virginia, and "Samson" recently moved to Cleveland, Ohio; Erie was within driving distance for all of them. Jerry, a missionary in Romania, had only attended the reunions when he was in the States. This year, he was flying in from Boise, ID, where his sending church was located.

As Brandon drove up, he noticed the house looked attractive and well-maintained. He thought it would do nicely for their three-day get-together. He knew Smitty had done his research well and had some activities for them to do in the area.

Brandon jumped out of the car and gave his buddy a bear hug. "Am I the first one to get here?"

"Well, yes, you're first after me!" replied Smitty. "The other two won't get here until after dinner. Looks like you and I will be christening the kitchen this evening. Did you bring your recipes and your special pan?"
"You bet I did," retorted Brandon. "I wouldn't want to eat your cooking, let alone the other guys' feeble attempts!"

"I don't blame you, Brandon. Let me help you with your things."

After the two men got Brandon's bag and his favorite cooking gear into the house, Brandon went right to work on their supper. But they were able to catch up as he worked.

Too Busy

"We are so excited about what God is doing to reach our community through our church people!" exclaimed Smitty as he watched his friend deftly slice onions and peppers and toss them into the frying pan.

"Really? Great. Tell me about what you're doing," Brandon responded, afraid his uneasiness showed more than he intended.

Smitty didn't seem to notice. Instead, as Brandon dazzled him with his cooking skills, he said, "I'd love to!" and then continued. "We're seeing progress with our people sharing the gospel with others and bringing them to Christ in a lot of different ways. Back when we started planting this church four years ago, Jenny and I determined that it had to be us, pastor and wife, who would lead and drive the ministry of evangelism by example."

Now Brandon always could cook without thinking about it. In fact, one of the reasons he loved to cook was that he enjoyed thinking through sermons and lessons he was preparing while he was cooking. So that wasn't why he was struggling to listen to Smitty as he carried on about the abundant new growth they were seeing at their now established church. It was that first statement, *"...it had to be us, pastor and wife, who would lead and drive the ministry of evangelism by example."*

As Brandon continued to mix, stir, and combine ingredients, he finally admitted to himself: *This is why I'm so frustrated. Sure, I preach the gospel. Yes, I believe that every believer, including myself, should be sharing his faith, but I have to admit that it just isn't happening in my own life.*

And while I'm conceding the fact that I'm not personally involved in evangelism, I might as well own up to the fact that my church isn't reaching people either. We're doing ministry. I think people are growing. Our worship is powerful; our missions-giving is robust. But are we really reaching out and bringing people to Christ?

Brandon could hear Smitty going on over his shoulder, but as he absentmindedly put the finishing touches on their meal, he continued pondering his dilemma. *But we are evangelistic, aren't we? We run a mean*

Vacation Bible School every summer. Our Christmas and Easter musicals are evangelistic. He stopped himself from continuing his grocery list of ministries. *No, those programs, as good as they might be, are not producing new converts. We're not growing. We're not evangelistic. Fact is, I'm not evangelistic, so how can I expect my church to be. Maybe it's time I admit this not only to myself, but also let someone else in on this, confide in someone.*

"You know," Brandon responded slowly as he arranged the finished meal on two plates. "I'm afraid I'm not involved much in personal evangelism." He let the words hang in the air a moment before he added, "But I'm so busy with trying to carry out the ministry of the church that I just don't see when I would fit it in!"

Oh brother! he thought, *What a cop-out!*

But he continued speaking, "It's true, with sermon preps, Sunday School, deacons' meetings, hospital visits, committee meetings, building projects, counseling—I don't have time for evangelism. I've got to spend some time with my family, you know. I've been thinking about adding an outreach pastor."

Did I really just say that to one of my closest friends? Brandon thought. *Can't I be honest with him?*

"Smitty, this is hot and ready, so could you lead us in prayer?"

"Sure," replied Smitty, salivating and rubbing his hands together. He prayed a simple prayer of thanksgiving, and they enjoyed their food while catching up about their wives and kids. Though they hadn't resumed the prior conversation, Brandon was determined he would bring it up again. Something needed to change; he was sure of that, and if he couldn't confide in one of his closest friends, then what could he do?

"Hey, listen, Smitty," he began. "When you mentioned that you and Jenny had determined that you needed to lead the evangelism ministry at your church by example, that really hit me. You know, I want to share the gospel; I want to be an example to my people, but I struggle.

"I'd like to reach my neighbors and have always had the best intentions," his voice trailed off as he formed his thoughts. After a brief pause, he continued.

"For example, back when I was a youth pastor in Williamsport, I wanted to witness to my neighbors but never got around to it. I made excuses to myself that since I didn't do it early on, it would be awkward to try to broach the subject later. So, when we moved to our next church, I was determined to start out early talking with neighbors around me and sharing my faith so it would be natural. But as I began to meet them, I didn't want to scare people away, so I always thought, 'Next time. Next time, I'll get into a spiritual conversation.' Well, time got away from me, and before I knew it, we were moving to our present location, thinking the same thing: 'Here I'll start out early talking about spiritual things in everyday conversations. Then it'll be natural, and I'll be able to witness effectively.' But the same thing happened, I felt so busy jumping into my new role that I never really got around to it. And now it's been, what, three years in our 'new' place, and I've still not started one spiritual conversation with anyone in our neighborhood. Oh, I'm a wimp! From the pulpit, I can preach up a storm. In my backyard . . ." Brandon let the statement remain unfinished.

Smitty let out a long sigh. Then he comforted his friend, "I hear you, Brandon. I've faced some of those same fears. In fact, I'm surprised how you've articulated so well what I experienced but never told anyone. Anyone but Jenny, that is. We were able to kind of spur each other on when we started in Huntington. Maybe it was because we were starting from scratch and feeling all alone, but we just began to prod each other and ask how we were doing. What a great help she was to nudge me along in my evangelism efforts! That and praying together that God would use us to reach people."

"Wow, that's cool," Brandon responded. "I'm glad you and Jenny could keep each other accountable like that. I'm sure Rebekah would be helpful, too, but it's been," he stopped to count in his head, "it's been nearly 10 years since I've had a good, solid gospel conversation with someone outside of church or a hospital. What's wrong with me. I mean really, what kind of pastor am I?"

Thoughts from the Good Soil Team

Brandon is not alone. Many believers, leaders, and even pastors are sensing the same problem in their lives. In fact, you may be feeling some of the same frustrations. Ten years may not have passed since you shared the gospel one-on-one, but you may have to admit that you have not been as evangelistic as you could be or should be. You may not be modeling an evangelistic fervor and lifestyle like you should. Maybe

Gaining Ground as a Truly Evangelistic Church

your church is not evangelistic—it's not reaching out as it should—and you'd like to see that change.

We'll see how Brandon and Smitty address the problem, but there is also an issue weighing heavily on another of the four friends. Let's meet the other two colleagues and learn what that concern is.

Reunion

Eli and Jerry got in late that night, so after a short round of small talk and getting settled, they all hit the hay. Brandon was up early preparing 'Eggs Brandon' for the crew.

Eli Donnella, lovingly referred to as "Samson" by his comrades, could still be heard snoring away at the other end of the house. Brandon smiled as he remembered their reunion the night before. His solid 6' 5" frame of 265 pounds had gained him the moniker of Samson, and he still looked like he did in college—his hair a little shorter and a bit gray around the edges—but still looked like he could hold his own on the football field.

Jerry Taine was already stirring in the next room. Again, Brandon smiled, wondering if it was Samson's snoring that awakened Jerry. His return flight from Romania with his family for this furlough had only taken place a little over a month ago. Now he had flown from Boise to Pittsburgh (instead of directly to Erie to save $300!) and driven a rental car the remaining 120 miles. *He must be worn out*, marveled Brandon.

All four of them were together again. They had missed their missionary friend at their last three reunions. Once more, Brandon smiled. *This is gonna be good.*

What's Stopping Us?

By 9:00, everyone was up and moving. Brandon beat the bottom of a pan. "Breakfast is ready; come and get it!" he shouted.

"You don't have to tell me twice," acknowledged Samson, bounding down the hallway of the little house. "I'm ready to eat!"

"You're always ready to eat," kidded Smitty. "How do you not get fat?"

"What do you mean?" he asked, flexing, and displaying several athletic poses. "It takes every bit of nourishment I put in this body God gave me to keep me moving and functioning the way He intended."

"Oh, brother," Jerry moaned, bringing up the rear. "Shall I pray and get this show on the road?"

After prayer, they all dug into the egg and sausage dish Brandon had prepared. As they ate, Smitty wanted to bring up the topic from the evening before, but he and Jerry spoke at the same time. Jerry took another bite and motioned for Smitty to go ahead.

"Well, Brandon and I were talking a bit about evangelism last night, and I want to ask, Jerry, how's it going with you guys over in Romania?" Smitty tried his best Romanian accent and waved his arms as he spoke.

Jerry responded, "I'd love to answer your question, but there's something that has been on my heart. Do you mind if I touch on that first?"

Now it was Smitty's turn to nod his assent as he enjoyed a bite of his breakfast.

"Thanks." Jerry took a deep breath and continued. "We've been back in the States for two furloughs now, and I don't know if it's just me, but I seem to have noticed in many of our churches a lack of evangelistic fervor which gets worse each time we're back."

Both Brandon and Smitty nearly dropped their forks and looked at each other, eyes wide. Neither spoke as Jerry carried on with his concern.

"I'm not sure what the root cause of this is—or if it even matters—but I've observed what I think could be several causes as I've visited our supporting churches. One is obvious, and it's been around forever – simple apathy. Other reasons could be that people fear rejection, don't know what to say, or even fear imposing their beliefs on others in a pluralistic society."

"But I think all of them can be dealt with by looking at the Thessalonian church. Even though the Thessalonians faced the fears I mentioned, they learned to imitate their pastor, who imitated Jesus Christ. Verse six says, 'and you became imitators of us and of the Lord.' A great way to become a Christian model, or pattern for others to emulate, is to imitate a godly mentor-model yourself. The Thessalonian Christians mimicked what they saw in Pastor Paul's life and became examples 'to all the believers in Macedonia and in Achaia,' so much so that the 'word of the Lord sounded forth'[1]—it echoed all over the area!"

"I know," interrupted Smitty with a sheepish grin on his face. "Me, being the jokester of the group, you'd think I'd grab onto this *mimic* idea—just like my dad who loved the way Rich Little used to impersonate celebrities years ago or more recently, Dana Carvey, or the way Darrell Hammond mimics Trump. But I know my Greek, too. I know this word 'imitators' comes from the Greek word *mimetes*, which was generally used in a more serious sense. How many times does it show up in the New Testament? Five or six? And it's always a positive imitation arising from admiring the pattern set by someone worthy of emulation."

Silence fell over the group. Everyone just looked at Smitty.

Trying to suppress a grin and giving a fake hurt look, he responded, "What? You think I didn't pay attention in Greek class or that I forgot everything I studied ten years ago? I am a pastor, too, you know. I preach and teach every week!"

The four erupted into laughter. When they settled down, it was Smitty who turned serious quickly. "You know, Brandon, I appreciate your openness and honesty last night about wanting to be more intentional not only in sharing your faith, but also in being an example to your people."

---

1. 1 Thessalonians 1:7-8

There it was, Brandon thought. *It is out to the other guys, too, and I didn't even get to bring it up. No time to worry about it now. Smitty's still talking. And these guys love me anyway. What's Smitty saying?*

"This passage kind of hits you—hits all of us—right where we are. Are we pastors who really want to fulfill our calling well? If so, we should imitate Christ as best we can, in all of his moral qualities and his compassion for sinners. Then, we need to do as Paul did, challenge our congregations to imitate us as we imitate Christ."

"Thanks, Smitty," Brandon answered quietly. "It would be a little bold for me to ask my church folks to imitate me at this point, but . . ."

Smitty interrupted, "Yes, that's being audaciously bold—for any of us. But it's being authentic."

"And you will find that others will follow if you practice what you preach," Samson encouraged. "Carolyn and I have found that even 'pew-warming' Christians who begin to see a Christlike example in their leaders develop a desire to be closer to God and more Christlike in their own lives among unbelievers."

"Yes," Smitty added, "didn't the writer of the letter to the Hebrews say to 'remember your leaders and imitate their faith?'"[2]

"Yep, Hebrews 13:7," answered Jerry. "And what's really exciting about all these lives being changed by the gospel and this imitating of models is that it spreads." They all had their Bibles out by now, dirty dishes pushed to the side or out in the kitchen. "Look at verse eight: 'For not only has the word of the Lord sounded forth from you in Macedonia and Achaia, but your faith in God has gone forth everywhere, so that we need not say anything.'"

Smitty chimed in, "Hey, that's like free advertising for your church!"

"Wow," acknowledged Brandon quietly. "This is powerful."

He paused, thinking through all his three friends had shared over the last 20 minutes. Changed lives . . . imitating . . . modeling . . . echoing. That's what he wanted for his own life and for his church.

---

2 "Remember your leaders, those who spoke to you the word of God. Consider the outcome of their way of life, and imitate their faith." Hebrews 13:7.

"I do so want to be a pastor (dare I say an evangelist?), that my people can imitate. I want changed lives which can be patterns for others and which 'sound forth' the word of the Lord."

What a great start to their retreat! Brandon couldn't have asked for anything better. Although both he and Smitty were committed to getting back to how Brandon could become more evangelistic himself and see his church do the same, they knew that would transpire over the weekend as the four close friends continued to share and encourage one another. But for now, the four prayed together and then cleaned up the dishes.

Thoughts from the Good Soil Team

Now, let's follow the guys as they uncover some essential elements of a truly evangelistic church--those things which pastors and members must do if the church is to be reaching new disciples. If they can determine what these key elements are, then they can take steps toward making them happen and trust God to effect change.

First Things First

After a delightful time of prayer and with a sparkling kitchen behind them which Brandon thought would make his wife proud, the guys plopped down on the couch and stuffed chairs in the living room of their rented Airbnb. Brandon was determined to start the conversation this time.

"Well, guys, I really appreciated our discussion about the story of the Thessalonian church—it's really helping me already with what I was chatting with Smitty about last night." He took a deep breath and let it out. *Here goes*, he thought.

"My church is not echoing the gospel as it should be. But the fact is that I've come to realize that *I* have not been faithful in sharing the gospel as I should. I have not been an example to my people. I have not been 'sounding forth' the word. Oh, maybe my life does some sounding forth because Jesus changed my life, but I'm not opening my mouth and personally telling others about Jesus. I'm certainly not echoing the gospel in that way. I'm determined to change that, but I'd like some help."

Nods and brief words of affirmation came from each of the guys, but Brandon continued.

"Last night before I lay down on my bed, I knelt beside it and confessed my failure to God. It's amazing how much lighter I feel this morning! 'He is faithful and just to forgive us,' right?"

"Amen," was shouted in unison by the three listeners.

"But I don't want the weight of responsibility to be lifted. I don't want to let this moment be lost and not take steps to reverse my actions—or inaction in this case! So, I'd appreciate all the help you can give me. Just before we started talking about 'the Echo Church,' Smitty had asked Jerry about how the evangelism efforts were going with his group in Romania. I'd like to hear from Jerry, really from all of you: How are you making headway in evangelism with your people?"

Jerry responded eagerly, "Sure, I'd be glad to interact on this. But listen, we struggled at first to get our people actively sharing the gospel. Believe it or not (it shouldn't be surprising based on our breakfast discussion), it was our example that made the difference. Our international team (missionaries and Romanian pastors) in Romania believes the pastor—and if there is more than one, the senior pastor—must model, lead, and advance the ministry of evangelism. It is too important to ignore or to delegate to someone else.

"I first saw the importance of this when I was an intern before we went to Romania. Remember that church in Ohio where we spent a year at the end of our partner-raising time? That pastor modeled this for me. Although he was pastoring a church of 1200 people, he always made time to be with unbelievers, investing in them, sharing his life . . . and his faith. The people in the church saw that and followed his example. I determined I would do the same."

Brandon let out a low whistle. He was clearly thinking about what he had just heard. Jerry waited, letting him form his thoughts into a response.

After a few seconds, Brandon commented, "Wow! In our church of 200, I'm having trouble just finding time to prepare to preach and keeping up with the ministries we have going. You're a missionary (you don't have much going on), but how did your pastor of such a big church find time to do evangelism?"

"Is that what you think?" Jerry responded laughing heartily. "I don't have much going on?"

"Come on, you know what I mean, you're starting a church. You don't have all the programs to deal with like we do."

"Well, maybe I can fill you in later about what we have 'going on,' but first, let me answer your question about Pastor Ernst. Even though he was pastoring a large church, he maintained the priority of personal evangelism and discipleship. He believed that the senior pastor had to lead by example. So, because of that, some supposedly great ideas were shot down in favor of keeping the main thing the main thing.

"So that's what we did in Romania, too. Right from the beginning we determined that each of us—no matter what developed and no matter what possibilities came our way—each of us missionary pastors would always make time and preserve energy for evangelism and discipleship. That didn't mean we had to do it all, but simply that we did do it."

"Hear, hear!" encouraged Samson. "You guys are familiar with our inner-city church in Cleveland. We've got a ton of programs going on—maybe too many—but I try to maintain personal evangelism and discipleship as a priority." Then he grunted, "Hmph," thinking back. "A couple of years ago, because we were growing and I had so much to do, I tried to *delegate* evangelism to one of my staff members. I thought I'd make him the evangelism pastor and watch our church take off while I, relieved of that responsibility, could concentrate on other things."

"That sounds good," Brandon interrupted.

"But it wasn't," Samson countered, shaking his head. "When people didn't see me doing evangelism, didn't hear my stories about successes and failures, didn't hear me talking about it from the pulpit, then they didn't seem to see the need. They weren't convinced of its importance."

"Wow, really?" Brandon was surprised.

"Yeah, I was surprised, too," continued Samson. "I mean, that's what you do, right? Add a staff member; let the senior pastor study and preach! But we started going backwards. As soon as I noticed the change, I talked with the deacons. One wise deacon asserted, "It must be the senior pastor who leads the church in evangelism. He must model it for the sheep, or they will not get it."

Good Shepherd

Brandon was trying hard to learn from his friends. He blurted out, "So, what does that look like?"

Quietly, simply, the answer came: "It looks like the Good Shepherd."

"What do you mean, Smitty?"

"You remember that well-known painting—what was the guy's name, Soud, Soord—whatever. But the shepherd is on the edge of a cliff, reaching down to get the lost sheep who is in danger. That's what it looks like."

"Sure," continued Jerry, "the pastor (shepherd) is out there, like Jesus, putting his life on the line seeking to rescue lost sheep."

Samson added, "And not only is that emulating Christ's actions and attitudes, but it also follows what Paul insisted a pastor should do. He told his mentee, Timothy, to do the work of an evangelist as one of his duties of a pastor.

"You know," he continued, "when I got back to modeling what it's like to be a good shepherd, trying to snatch sheep from danger, my people started getting on board."

"I know what you mean, Samson," Smitty rejoined, "but I discovered that I also had to talk about it. I share with people personally and from the pulpit the victories and the struggles. That sharing encourages people that they're not alone in this, and it motivates them to be diligent."

Building a Team

"So, guys," Brandon said, "I have to admit I have not been modeling evangelism for my church. In fact, as you know, I've been pastoring for years, but you may not have known that I've always struggled with evangelism. You guys have been an inspiration (and a challenge) to me. I'm going to make time and discipline myself to do better. Then I should see our plateaued church grow again."

"Now that's exciting to hear," Smitty encouraged, "However, I found that modeling was simply the spark to get people interested. I also needed to lead them in evangelism which required *training* and being *involved* with them in the task."

"That's right," Samson continued. "Every pastor on our staff—no matter what pastoral role they have—makes time and is involved in personal evangelism."

Jerry piled on. "I've also found that as I'm trying to lead in evangelism I need to get buy-in from others, too."

"Okay, okay, I get it. I didn't mean to sound so simplistic or that I thought it would be easy," countered Brandon. "It will take a lot more than just modeling. But now I'm curious, Jerry, what do you mean by 'buy-in'?"

"Well, lay leadership buy-in is crucial," Jerry responded. "This is the pastor's first and possibly most challenging task. This didn't originate with me; it's something else I learned in my internship with Pastor Ernst."

"I agree," added Samson. "That's why I spend so much time with a group I call Pew Leadership. You know, we still have those beautiful old wooden pews in our building! Pew Leadership are leaders—sometimes just your average Joes and Janes—who are carrying the torch for evangelism in our church. I'd like to come up with a different name, but I used that early on and it stuck."

"Yep," continued Jerry, "this leadership among peers (not the pastor or leader of the church) adds credibility to the pastor's leadership in such a crucial task as personal evangelism. That's why I spent so much time with the core of our church plant early on. I gave these guys and gals the name of *Campioni de evanghelizare*—Evangelism Champions. I gave them that name not necessarily because they were great at it—champions—but because they championed the cause."

"Hey, that has a nice ring to it," Samson approved. "Do you mind if I use that?"

"Not at all," responded Jerry. "The point is, Brandon, that people in the 'pew' can think that evangelism is just the pastor's job."

"Or that he's the only one who can do it," added Smitty. "After all, he is trained theologically. He's the professional."

"The fact is," Jerry continued, "in many places overseas, being a pastor creates a barrier—people aren't as likely to allow a pastor to get close to them."

"Overseas?" questioned Brandon. "I have experienced that here in the States."

"I think we all do," Samson agreed. "But everyday church members have natural networks of unbelieving friends, coworkers, neighbors, and relatives who know and trust them. When we build into their lives and they imitate our Good Shepherd-ness, they become Pew Leadership—*Campi . . . Campion . . .*—you know, Evangelism Champions!"

"But how do you develop pew leadership or *Campioni de evanghelizare*?" Brandon queried.

"*Hei, bine făcut!* Well done!" Jerry complimented his friend."

"Well, you know, I'm a quick learner."

"So, the first thing you need to do is look for members who you think will have the potential of being an evangelism champion. Don't worry about getting a lot of them, maybe even just one or two; a small, committed group is better than a big group that doesn't end up being champions after all."

"What do I look for in these people? How will I know they'll be committed?"

"Well," answered Samson, then paused. "People who are asking for prayer for their lost friends and loved ones, to start."

"Sure," agreed Smitty, "and look for people who are already sharing stories about someone they are trying to reach and inviting people to special events."

"Yep," continued Jerry, "We also look for those who are living out their Christian lives consistently and boldly where they work and respond eagerly when we offer training. These people have great potential to be *Campioni de evanghelizare*."

Samson carried the torch forward. "Now, once you discover some of these people, you would want to meet with them and share about your desire to form a team, right? That's what I did with the Pew Leadership."

"Yes, we met with them, prayed together, and gave them a book. Well, I gave them a pdf of my translation of Robert Coleman's little book *The Master Plan of Evangelism*. Then we trained the ones that kept coming back. As they got more involved in reaching their friends and family, others couldn't help but catch the fever. Our Champions championed the cause of personal evangelism among other church members. Then, eventually we just changed the name of the group to *Echipa de Evanghelizare* or *Echipa E.*"

Smitty commented sarcastically, "Oh, that makes sense!" Then added, "Uh, what does that mean?"

Jerry responded, "*Echipa de Evanghelizare* is Evangelism Team or E-Team. We switched because 'champion' was giving some people the idea that they had to be champions at evangelism or really good at it. The original intention was just that they championed evangelism; they did it; they encouraged it. E-Team gets that across without the confusion."

"E-Team. I like it," Samson commented.

Breakfast had been gone for some time. Most of the conversation had taken place while leaning back on two legs of their chairs and picking chia seeds (a secret, healthy, protein-adding ingredient in Brandon's breakfast dish) out of their teeth. With satisfied appetites—physical and spiritual—the guys were ready to head to Presque Isle for some fun in the sun and sand.

Smitty gave instructions for an on-time departure for the beach, teeth were brushed, swimsuits donned, lunch packed in the cooler, and the car loaded. As they headed out the door to pile into Jerry's rental, Brandon commented, "Seems like we all were enjoying the topic of conversation." Then he asked, "Do you mind if we keep exploring this theme throughout our time here?"

Bottom Line

Jerry got behind the wheel, and after pushing the front seat all the way back, Samson folded himself into the passenger's side. Smitty got in behind Jerry; Brandon, knees almost in his chest squeezed behind Samson. Fortunately, the Airbnb was ideally located, so in only 10 minutes, the guys were peeling themselves back out of the vehicle.

"So, Brandon," Samson began, stretching his back, "this 'theme' you wanted to continue to explore, put it into a couple of sentences—what are we talking about?"

"Well, like I said," Brandon responded, "I haven't been sharing the gospel personally as I should, nor I'm afraid—like pastor, like flock—are my people. I'm wondering what it would take for my church to become truly evangelistic."

"Oh, okay, something simple then!" Smitty chimed in with as straight and serious a face as only he could pull off. The laughter which followed made it obvious they understood his sarcasm. What's new? They had been dealing with Smitty's satirical manner for over 10 years.

As they unloaded the car and walked from the parking lot to the beach, the conversation continued. Brandon ventured, "All right, all right. I realize it may be a tall order, but what might make a difference? Are there any key things that I can do, some essential steps that, if taken, would ensure our church would be truly evangelistic? Or any church for that matter—small churches, big churches, country churches, city churches, churches being planted, churches with one foot in the grave. Shouldn't there be some principles that work any and everywhere?"

Smitty whistled. "Tall order? Naw, piece of cake."

Samson thrust the point of the "sun-brella" into the sand and lifted the supports until he heard the familiar click. He spread out a beach towel underneath and plopped down, all the while pensive. His friends were expecting something profound.

"That would be great, wouldn't it?" he started slowly. "A silver bullet, a magic bean, a cure-all."

Jerry got on board. "An elixir, a wonder drug, a nostrum."

Smitty couldn't resist. "A panacea, a catholicon, a theriac."

"A what?" Brandon asked. "I got the gist pretty early on, but you lost me with 'theriac.'"

"It was the name of this free e-book I got on Amazon—spooky! I didn't finish it." Everyone laughed. "But the idea is the same—a one-size-fits-all remedy. Samson spoke again. "I'm not sure there are 'six easy steps' to being an evangelistic church, or a . . ." after a dramatic pause, "a theriac to fix your church, but I believe if we put our heads together, we could figure out something. Some . . . essential elements . . . that could make a difference if they were to be found in a body of believers seeking to fulfill the Great Commission."

"That's it!" Brandon shot back. "A church's mission—THE mission the church pursues above all else must be the Great Commission."

"You mean the church must be missions-minded?" asked Smitty.

"Nope, but it must be mission-minded; not just sending missionaries around the world, which it should be doing, but focused—more than anything else—on the mission of the church, to make disciples."

Jerry piped up with, "Okay, I'll bite. How does a church get to be mission-minded? Let's see if we can tear into this and make it a practical exercise." Samson and Jerry grabbed a football and tossed it back and forth as they talked. Smitty and Brandon threw a frisbee.

"So, let's start with Matthew 28:18-20," Samson gave a lopsided grin. "Say it

Gaining Ground as a Truly Evangelistic Church

with me, class." Everyone chimed in:

"And Jesus came and said to them, 'All authority in heaven and on earth has been given to me. Go therefore and make disciples of all nations, baptizing them in the name of the Father and of the Son and of the Holy Spirit, teaching them to observe all that I have commanded you. And behold, I am with you always, to the end of the age."

Samson finished with, "Thank you, kids," and fired a bullet pass to Jerry. Then he stated, "Okay, that's the Great Commission—one version of it. So, how do we know if a church is making it *their* mission?"

Passes went back and forth; the frisbee flew and floated; thoughts raced. Finally, Jerry spoke, "What does 'Go' mean?"

Smitty, incredulously ventured, "Um, really?"

Jerry came back with, "Yes, we all know that 'Go' is not the main verb of the passage, but a participle which could mean, 'having gone' or 'when you have gone.' But I believe this is a participle of 'attendant circumstance' which has the force of a verbal command: 'Go!' Jesus desires believers will go to those without Christ. So, really the first question we can ask is this: 'Are the people actively going like Jesus intended?'"

"Hmph." Samson added, "One kind of wonders if they—the original disciples—got the idea at first because they were all staying in Jerusalem, but by Acts chapter 8, after a persecution had arisen, we see people scattered who 'went about preaching the word.' It seemed to be kind of a natural thing. In Acts 11:19 we see the same thing: those scattered because of the persecution were 'speaking the word' as they went."

"Right!" answered Brandon. "We should be able to ask if people are out there—in the world—actively engaging unbelievers." Then, less enthusiastically, he added, "I know I haven't been doing that like I should. And if we are talking about what Jesus has done for us, then new people should be showing up in church either because they have come to Christ or they are curious and want to know more."

"So, it seems," pondered Samson out loud, "that if we were creating a litmus test of a Great Commission church, we ought to be able to ask, "Is this church actively 'going' in the way Jesus intended in His commission?"

Nods, smiles, grunts of affirmation.

Smitty spoke up. "Well, I hate to be too obvious, but wouldn't the next question be, 'Are they making disciples?'"

Samson responded, "I think so, but we're talking about making followers of Jesus, right? I mean, Jesus says to make disciples and the next thing he says—the next step in the process—is to baptize them. I think the emphasis here is being in the world (not of it) and bringing people to believe in and follow Jesus. Then you dunk them!"

Jerry tossed the ball back and agreed, "I think I know what you mean. Discipleship has come to mean one-on-one or group Bible studies, which of course, is all good. But a major part of making disciples is *reaching* them first: being out there, seeing people trust in Jesus. Then you baptize them, and then you teach them."

"And that's where what we so often think of discipleship comes in—with the teaching," Samson added.

"So, we're all agreed that a major part of 'making disciples' is actually bringing people to Christ first?" asked Brandon.

"Yep, it's really more about evangelism than the modern meaning of discipleship seems to include," affirmed Samson.

"Cool. But I'm hot," moaned Smitty with a smirk. "Let's hit the water."

Global Missions?

All his life, Brandon tended to get out of the water before anyone else. At 5'10" and 155 pounds, he figured it was simply because he didn't have enough meat on his bones to keep him warm. Shivering, he trotted to the edge of the water, then walked up to where their things were sprawled out on the sand, and opened the cooler. He spread a tablecloth and began to set out their lunch. As he did, he thought through what he and his longtime friends had been saying.

He thought to himself, *First, I've got to be bolder and persistent in my witness. I need to model it for my people. Then, I need to build an E-Team, people who are doing it with me and helping others see God at work, so they'll want to get on board. That should move our church toward being evangelistic as a body: going—being out there with people making disciples, baby Christ-followers who will be baptized and brought into the church.*

But something was bothering him—again. As he laid the fruit out with everything else and prepared to call the guys 'to the table,' he mumbled Matthew 28: 19 to himself, "'Go therefore, and make disciples of all nations . . .'" *Is this just a missions verse after all? Was Jesus simply saying that disciples were to be made around the world? After all, Jesus' Great Commission as recorded in Acts 1:8 says to go to the end of the earth making disciples. And the Luke 24 passage says that repentance in Jesus' name should be "proclaimed to all nations." Ah,* Brandon argued with himself, *but it should be done "beginning in Jerusalem." They weren't to preach anywhere else until they had started in Jerusalem.*

"Hey guys, come and get it!" Brandon yelled toward Lake Erie. The guys responded quickly and were drying off and getting settled in no time.

"Hey, I've got a question for you geek scholars, I mean Greek scholars," Brandon joked, then asked Samson to lead in prayer.

After offering a simple prayer of gratefulness, Samson asked, "What's up?"

Brandon voiced his ponderings. "There in Matthew 28:19, when Jesus said to make disciples of every nation, do you think that he meant we needed to go around the world making disciples?"

"Well, yes," Samson responded quickly. "And no," he added. "*Panta ta ethne* (of all nations) refers to ethnicities, extended families, languages that make up the peoples of the earth. Ralph Winter and Donald MacGavern quite famously used this interpretation to introduce the idea of reaching 'hidden peoples' instead of thinking of going past country boundaries. Since then, Piper and Platt have emphasized the need to take the gospel to 'unreached people groups.'[3]

Why do you ask?"

"So, Matthew 28:19-20—all the Great Commission verses—aren't necessarily missions verses only—intending for us to go across borders? *Panta ta ethne* could be referring to people from different groups who are actually right next door or across the street?"

Starting to talk with a full mouth, then swallowing and continuing, Smitty commented, "Wow, this is getting deep! But really..." Here Smitty paused, put his food down thoughtfully, and continued. "When Jesus shared those words, I don't think the Jews around him were thinking of 'the nations' in a modern socio-anthropological sense, but I don't think they were thinking of nations with borders either. They were thinking of unbelieving 'strangers' all around them. They would have been thinking of non-believing Gentiles as Isaiah referred to them in Isaiah 66 and the non-Jews Paul later spoke of as 'separated from Christ' and 'strangers to the covenants of promise' in Ephesians 2."

Samson tracked right along with Smitty. He added, "So, missions? Yeah, the Great Commission verses are missions challenges, but they are more than that. Jesus wanted His followers to start by reaching out to strangers, or unbelievers, all around them—right there in Jerusalem and Judea—and then crossing borders to reach unbelievers all over the world."

"So," surmised Brandon, "it includes my Filipino neighbors next door, and the Nepalese family across the street from one of my deacons..."

"...and the Iraqis living on my block," Samson finished. "I'm curious, are your

---

3 Darren Carlson and Elliot Clark, "The 3 Words That Changed Missions Strategy—and Why They Might Be Wrong," https://www.thegospelcoalition.org/article/misleading-words-missions-strategy-un-reached-people-groups/

churches reaching the *panta ta ethne* around you? Cleveland is 51% Black, 34% White, 10% Hispanic and 2% Asian. Our church almost hits those same percentages. But we are missing pockets of immigrants moving in from Asia. We want to start reaching them, too, by helping our church people befriend them in their neighborhoods."[4]

Smitty had been doing the math in his head (and with his fingers!) and was ready to share. "You know we went to start a church in Huntington concentrating on the Asian population. We're running just under 100 right now. Twenty-three are of Asian descent, about 10 are African American, and about the same Hispanic."

"I have to confess," admitted Brandon, "that we are almost completely monocultural. We're going to need to do a better job of seeking out 'the nations' around us."

"We can certainly all do a better job and pray for one another," Samson encouraged. "The *panta ta ethne* (all nations) of which we are to make disciples are non-believing people and people groups all around us and all around the world. But we clearly need to start with the ones nearest to us, in our Jerusalem..."

"...and not stop until we get to the Romanians, Ukrainians, Cambodians, and Zimbabweans of the world," added Jerry.

---

4 EveryEthne can help your church members reach "the nations" around them. Read here about their vision: Our passion is to be on mission with the Church to reach EveryEthne in North America through a disciple-making movement that multiplies leaders and churches. This initiative is focused on seeing the Church **advance, mobilize** and **multiply.**

We offer churches a library of resources and tools to help them continue to grow spiritually, multiply, reach their community, develop leaders, and make disciples who make disciples. In particular, our demographic studies "paint a picture of your community's lostness". Our desire is to help you identify and own the lostness of your culturally, socially and religiously diverse community so that every man, woman, and child has repeated opportunities to hear, see and respond to the Gospel. Our team has more than a century of pastoral and church planting experience. Consider the benefits for you and your church by engaging with us. For more information about EveryEthne, contact us at info@ EveryEthne.church or visit our website www.EveryEthne.church.

The Main Thing

Having eaten way too much, the quartet lay on their towels, sleepy and content. Actually, some were fading in and out of sleep when Brandon brought them back to the topic at hand. "So, our litmus test for evangelistic churches starts with people 'going' or, in other words, being with non-believing people all around them, making disciples of them . . ."

"Which means bringing them to Jesus," Smitty interrupted.

"Right, bringing them to Jesus, and then baptizing and teaching them," Brandon finished.

"Exactly!" shouted Jerry, popping up off his towel. "I know too many missionaries overseas and churches in the States for that matter, that stop with 'decisions.' Followers of Jesus," he cocked his head and said under his breath, "(read 'disciples') are identified with Christ and His Church through baptism. It's part of the command already!"

"Down, boy, down!" Samson chided as all chuckled at Jerry's outburst. Then he continued, "Yeah, true disciples are going to be baptized, and a truly evangelistic church will be seeing people baptized and taught."
"So, we're saying that part of becoming a disciple is being baptized?" confirmed Jerry.

Smiling, Samson reiterated, "Yes, being baptized is part of becoming a disciple. But I think the key thing we've hit on today is that the church does not get sidetracked from THE mission of the church which is, and everybody said . . ."

All chiming in, "The Great Commission!"

"We've got to keep focused," added Smitty, "on that principal command Jesus gave us."

Samson quietly continued, "A pastor of a large church in our neck of the woods—one who is clearly concentrated on making disciples—told me that a well-known apologist asked if he could speak in their church on a Sunday morning. I remember thinking, *Wow! What an opportunity.* The pastor then told me he turned them down. At first, I thought he was crazy. Then he told me, 'It distracts from our mission.' I realized that here was a pastor and church who are so laser-focused on the mission that they would give up a great opportunity simply because it could get them sidetracked from their mission. That's what I want my church to be like; turning down the good, the really good, to keep focused on the best, THE mission of making disciples."

Far-Sighted

"I didn't know you wore glasses, Smitty! When did this happen?" asked Brandon.

"I don't. These are just for my presbyopia," answered Smitty.

"What? I thought you were a Baptist preacher." Samson entered the conversation late as he came down the hall shirtless, drying off after his shower. The guys had come back from Presque Isle Beach and were preparing to go out for the evening.

"Ho, ho, aren't you the funny one?!" Smitty mocked. Then, as from a dictionary, he quoted, "Presbyopia: farsightedness caused by loss of elasticity of the lens of the eye, occurring typically in middle and old age—watch it on the old age comments! My doctor told me a couple of months ago that what I'm dealing with is common. I just use these glasses for small print when reading a book or when I'm on the internet."

"So, what are you doing anyway?" asked Jerry.

"I'm looking up the best restaurant in Erie. Tonight is Brandon's night off from cooking and I wanted to 'focus'—see what I did there?—on the local cuisine if we could. The restaurant at the top of the list when Googling best restaurants in Erie is called *Give a Crêpe, La Creperie.* Their slogan is 'Giving a Crêpe about Erie.' I think that's where we ought to go."

"Well, I'm still feeling full from breakfast and lunch, so going light sounds good to me," Jerry agreed. "I don't know how we can do any better than Brandon's cooking anyway."

With the guys looking better (and smelling better), they piled into the car again to go the short distance down Peach Street to what at least some of the locals considered Erie's best restaurant. Its small size concerned them, but as they entered, the aroma calmed their fears. This should be good, thought Brandon, the connoisseur of the bunch. The fact is, the others were all meat-and-potatoes kind of guys, but they were willing to give it a try to please their foodie buddy. Besides, their *"presbyopian"* friend had found it for them, and Smitty was as basic when it came to eating as the next guy.

Glocal

Everyone ordered a savory crêpe (or two—what happened to eating light?) and was looking forward to a sweet one for dessert later. As the quartet waited for their savory dishes to come, Brandon's brow furrowed, then he observed, "You know, all this talk about presbyopia and not seeing well up close, got me to thinking: I wonder if my church has presbyopia."

"How do you mean, Brandon?" questioned Samson.

"Well, I've not been the best example, I know. But last November, for our missions conference, I scheduled some evangelism and discipleship training—I didn't plan a traditional conference with a keynote speaker, etc. Instead, I thought the training would be good for a missions conference. You know, like we were talking about this afternoon, getting us to think Great Commission but with a local focus. But I was highly criticized. I mean, everyone in the church has been so good to us and even past the honeymoon stage, people continue to demonstrate they like us..."

"Now *that* is amazing!" interjected Smitty.

Brandon, nonplussed at first, but not wanting to lose his thought, continued, "Even though things are great, that was a bit of a tenuous time. Continuing with the eyesight metaphors, I think our people are *far-sighted*—wanting to send missionaries around the world, but not wanting to focus on the people around us."

Jerry spoke up. "You won't find anyone more missions-minded than I; it's what I eat, sleep and breathe. But the local focus cannot be ignored. Each church's Jerusalem has got to be continually before them. In our church plants in Romania we are always trying to build a global concern into the DNA right from the beginning, but we think our core believers must clearly be concerned about making disciples around them first, or at least at the same time."

"Right," agreed Samson, "the opposite is no good either. We have a church in town which only has a local focus. Missions is completely off their radar. And while they do such a great job of building their ministry around a local focus, I can't help but think that they're missing something."

Smitty ventured, "Well, I don't think you're going to get an argument from any of us on keeping a balance between local and global ministry—glocal as it were. I mean, in Luke 24, Jesus starts His commission statement with, 'Beginning from Jerusalem' (where they were at the moment), and in Acts 1:8, His concentric circles challenge was to 'be my witnesses in Jerusalem (first again), *and* in all Judea, Samaria, *and* to the end of the earth.' But how can we keep that 'Here: There' ratio?"

"Hmm. Good question, Smitty," pondered Samson. "I don't think there is a tool or instrument which tells us for sure if we're perfectly balanced or teetering one way or the other. But I'll bet we could come up with questions to ask ourselves periodically: questions which could help our churches combat against presbyopia."

Jolene, their server, approached with a large tray balanced above her shoulder. "Presbyopia?" she asked. "Are you guys doctors or something?" As she quoted the contents of the plates which she proceeded to hand to the guys around the table, it was clear she had no interest in the answer. She quickly left the table with a smile and said, "Let me know if you need anything else."

After praying for the meal, Smitty pumped Samson, "Did you have any of those test questions in mind?"

"Actually, I did," answered Samson. After enjoying the first savory bite of his "Mr. Sir" crepe which included tarragon ham, gruyere, spinach, and béchamel, he continued, "Here's something we can consider: What percentage of our churches' programs are genuinely focused on spreading the gospel to our communities?"

"Yeah, that's a good touchstone," interjected Brandon. "And what if we asked, 'How much of our churches' budgets are allocated to local evangelistic outreach?'"

"Ooh, that's good," acknowledged Smitty. "I mean, how we spend our money isn't everything, but it can indicate what is important to us."

"And, speaking of percentages," echoed Samson, "what about this: What percentage—more or less—of church members are actively developing relationships with unbelievers with the goal of presenting the gospel to them as they show interest?"

Brandon came back with, "And how many lives of people living right around the church are being changed through the ministry of the church?"

Yeah, But

Jerry was listening intently as he enjoyed his crepe called simply "Savory." Its herbs de Provence and Amaro Alta Verde were perfectly blended. He put his fork down and commented, "These are great questions to determine if a church has a proper local focus. But last month when I was challenging one of our supporting churches to reach into their community, people complained, 'But you don't know how difficult it is to evangelize in our town. People here don't want to hear about God!'"

"Ouch!" winced Smitty. "How did you answer that?"

"I said, 'I see,'" responded Jerry. "Then I asked them, 'Where do you have missionaries serving, besides Romania where we are, of course?' After listing off several countries—many of which are difficult, slow-responding places in the world—I asked, 'Why are you sending missionaries there? Isn't it too hard there? You can't expect the missionaries to share the gospel where people don't want to hear about Jesus, can you?'

"I was getting nervous because I was being hard on them. I was concerned they might pull our support. But I finished with 'You see, Romans 1:16 tells us that the gospel is the power of God for salvation to everyone who believes. God can and does draw people to Himself even in difficult places. We need to trust Him and be faithful in sharing—wherever He places us in this world.'"

"How did they respond?" asked Brandon.

"Well, they're still supporting us, if that's what you mean," Jerry rejoined smiling. "But afterwards, several people also came up and thanked me for the challenge and asked me to pray that their church would gain more of a local focus."

We Can Do It!

"Cool!" exclaimed Samson, then added, "You know, I think there just may be a lot of churches out there who recognize or would be willing to recognize that they've lost their local focus and are concerned enough to take steps to regain it."

"Yeah, I suppose so," Smitty acknowledged. "What are you thinking?"

"I don't know," returned Samson. "But this whole topic Brandon got us going on yesterday about churches and individuals being evangelistic or not; it seems to be hitting a nerve. It's obviously important to Brandon (and I know he's not the only pastor who feels he's not reaching out personally as he should). It's tough for pastors to admit, but they know deep down it's true.

"And then there's this church that Jerry just mentioned. There are people and churches that are realizing they're not getting the job done and need help. Is there something we can do?"

"What do you mean?" Jerry interjected.

Samson continued. "Look, none of us are perfect, especially this lot! But God has blessed our ministries over the years, and as we've interacted on these concepts over the last two days, we've referred to ways we've seen God work and we've come up with ideas—some pretty good ones, too. I just wonder, if we put some thought and prayer and work into this, if we couldn't come up with some help for others facing these same issues."

"And," interrupted Jerry, "we are serving in some fairly diverse situations. You're inner city in Cleveland, Samson, with quite a mixed population. Smitty here is in West Virginia reaching an Asian population. I'm in Romania, representing missionary efforts overseas, and Brandon lives in upstate New York, basically in Anytown, USA. Some of the concepts we're learning and strategies we're using should apply to just about any situation."

"Especially if we work at staying biblical and generic in what we do, not trying to target any specific setting," agreed Samson.

"Interesting," Smitty reacted with no jokes, no puns, no sarcasm—unusual for him.

Everyone sat silently for a moment. Brandon, who of the crew had been most frustrated coming into their get-together, was sensing a breakthrough for himself and his church, and the exhilarating potential of help for others as well. If he were to be 100% honest, he would probably say he was about to jump out of his skin! This could transform his life and ministry. Finally, he spoke.

"Let's do it! Dessert is on me!" He called Jolene over, ordered the "Classic" sweet crepe (powdered sugar and fruit) all around, and asked, "Smitty, what are our plans for tomorrow?"

Smitty answered with exaggerated enthusiasm, "We are headed to Waldameer Park & Water World!" Everyone in the restaurant looked their way. Undaunted, probably even encouraged by the attention, he continued in mock TV show announcer style, "My extensive research revealed that Waldameer Park existed as early as the late 1800's as a picnic grove overlooking Lake Erie. (We passed it when we went to the beach today.) Erie Electric Motor Company developed the spot into a bona fide amusement park in the 1920s. Much has changed since then and now," (in dramatic voice again) "Waldameer Park & Water World is the biggest attraction for families in the Erie area with its over 100 rides, 19 waterslides, giant wave pool, and old fashioned Ferris wheel and merry-go-round!"

Spontaneous applause from Erie-ites in the restaurant erupted, and Smitty took a comical-looking bow while the others wished they could leave.

"Okay, that was . . . interesting," mumbled Jerry. "I forget what one can do in public in America which would never be dreamt of in Europe."

"Yes. Anyway," an embarrassed Brandon agreed, "I was wondering if we'd have any more time for our newly-agreed-upon project tomorrow. We're all heading home the day after."

"Right," responded Smitty. He continued quietly, "For all the hype," then more loudly and with fanfare, "and as wonderful as the park is," then quietly again, "it's not that big, so I figured we'll be done at the park by 3:30 or 4:00, get back to the house, eat, and pack for our trip the next day."

"So, we could easily spend some time on this tomorrow evening," Brandon conjectured.

"Yeah." "Sounds good!" "Great!" came the responses. "Let's plan on it."

As they enjoyed their dessert crepes and the guys joked and laughed together, Brandon thanked God again for these friends He had given him at university so many years ago. What a blessing they had been over the years! He couldn't help but think what a blessing they would be over the next months and years as they worked together on this new project.

That Was Fun!

"That was pretty cool for a local amusement park!" Jerry commented on their way back to the house from Waldameer Park & Water World.

"Yeah, the view of Lake Erie from the top of Ravine Flyer was beautiful," added Samson. "It's not everywhere you can see something like that."

"And the best part—no lines!" exclaimed Smitty. "And it was so compact; no getting lost in that park."

"Well, I really enjoyed The Whacky Shack," noted Brandon. "It reminded me of a 'dark ride' I experienced as a boy, well done, old-school."

"The amazing thing to me is that it is still running!" Interrupted Samson. "That thing looked like it's been there about a hundred years!"

"You may not be that far off," Smitty added. "Remember, the place was a picnic grove in 1896 which became an amusement park in the 1920's."

"So, Waldameer was fun, and we're heading back at," Jerry looked at his watch, "3:30. We ought to have plenty of time to do some work on our little project."

Brandon commented, "I cut up the tomatoes, lettuce, and onions and browned the hamburger this morning before we left. It's just a matter of putting the ingredients out and warming it up, and we'll each be able to put together our individual taco salads as we like."

As they rode in silence during the last five minutes of the trip back from the park, Brandon reminisced back over the time with his peers. Everything—their Presque Isle visit, the local restaurant, Waldameer with its crazy rides—had been a great time as usual. But what was emerging as a highlight from this trip were their times talking about how they could be more effective in evangelism and discipleship. He was eager for the upcoming interaction around the table once more.

What's Next?

With taco meat, onions, diced tomatoes, lettuce, and salsa all piled high on a bed of crunchy Fritos™ on their plates, the conversation erupted with everyone speaking at nearly the same time.

"We've got to plan some training."

"What we need to do is form a network."

"Accountability is going to be the key."

"Simplicity is paramount in staying on mission."

"Whoa! It's a shame no one is interested in this discussion," kidded Samson. "Let's start with a recap. First, we need a good shepherd-type pastor setting the example in evangelism and discipleship; he's doing it, investing time in lost sheep."

"That's number one," Smitty cheered.

Brandon jumped right in. "This good shepherd pastor has got to bring together a core of evangelism champions around him—an E-Team—who desire to make the Great Commission THE mission of the church. People need to be going, making disciples among different people groups who will be baptized and taught."

"Two and three," Smitty interjected again.

"But this emphasis of THE mission has to be done with a local focus— not just internationally," instructed Jerry.

"There's number four," observed Smitty.

"Hold on," interrupted Jerry. "Let me see if I can sort of map this out. After a few seconds, Jerry had the following scratched out on the legal pad he usually had with him for note-taking during his daily devotional time.

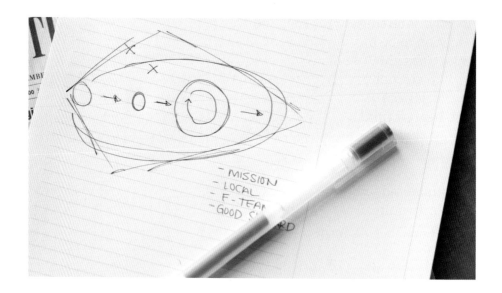

"Yeah, cool," Smitty commented.

"That's it," Samson added.

"So, I still think training needs to occur early in any kind of model that will produce a truly evangelistic church. We've got our pastor doing it, and he has people that are eager and trying—and maybe even doing it well. But what about the congregation? They're not equipped. We'd never send our soldiers to battle without proper training and effective resources."

"Excellent point!" raved Jerry. "And that's the pastor's job anyway, 'to equip the saints for the work of the ministry.'[5] You guys know that the Greek word for equip (*katartismos*), means to render effective and workable something that is not yet in a condition to function as it should."

"Well, if we didn't, we do now," joked Smitty. "Nice the way you pulled that right out of that geek head—I mean Greek head of yours."

Jerry admitted, "I just finished a study on this with my core four before coming back on furlough."

"Aha!" roared Smitty. "I didn't think you were *that* smart."

---

5 Ephesians 4:11-12. "And he gave the apostles, the prophets, the evangelists, the shepherds, and teachers, to equip the saints for the work of ministry..."

"Okay, okay," interrupted Samson, "but he is right. We can't expect the congregation to be involved in evangelism—or even the E-Team for that matter—unless they are equipped. And 'rendering effective and workable' people who are 'not yet in a condition to function as they should' is very clearly the pastors' job. We pastors need to take this verse and its key word, equip, to heart. I think we can extrapolate and determine that before this equipping takes place—whatever form it takes—the people *are not able to function as they should.*"

"Ouch," shuddered Smitty seriously. "That's alarming when you think about it. If we don't equip our people, they are not able to do what God wants them to do."

"And according to Jesus' final first century command," added Jerry, "God wants them to be making disciples."

Brandon let out a low whistle, then added, "Okeydokey," imitating one of his father's favorite affirmations. "Samson was right: training of the congregation—equipping as it were," he added with a nod to Jerry, "must be a priority."

"I think maybe we should call this essential *Equipped Congregation,*" Samson announced. "That matches the language of Ephesians."

"Cool!" "Sure," and "Makes sense," were the answers that came quickly in response.

Brandon started to collect the empty plates, and Samson followed his lead, lending a hand.

"Whew, that was great! Thanks, Brandon, for your great meal prep this whole time," Smitty encouraged. The others added their thanks.

"No problem," responded Brandon. "You know how I enjoy cooking." As he and Samson finished putting the dishes in the diminutive dishwasher—just right for this small crew—he asked, "So, what does 'equipping' look like in this context? What has to be done, and how do we do it?"

Jerry stood, stretched, and let out a yawn, more from being satisfied than from weariness. Then he commented, "Well, one thing I've learned from being in Europe and other cultures is that content and methods for Great

Commission equipping must change as culture changes."

"Hmm. Good point," agreed Samson. "And I think that would include not only moving from one culture to another but adapting methodology as any particular culture changes. I've found that methods and literature that were effective in our culture forty and fifty years ago no longer meet people where they are."

"You got that right," affirmed Smitty. "The evangelism methods we were trained in assumed the hearer had a basic knowledge of the Bible. After all, sixty years ago, when a lot of those tools were being developed, most people went to church, and nearly everyone had a basic understanding of the Bible. The people we're trying to reach in Huntington don't have a clue about who God is, what sin is, who Jesus is, or why he had to die—they don't even know basic Bible stories anymore."

"So, Great Commission equipping today needs to prepare disciple-makers to share the Bible's big story, giving people the historical-Biblical context necessary so that they can understand gospel truth," Jerry summarized.

"Well said," Brandon commented. "But won't that be difficult? Every believer is going to have to be a Bible scholar just to be able to engage unbelievers about Jesus."

"Not at all," disagreed Jerry. "They really just need to have a basic understanding of the Bible and its flow. And if the resources have the Biblical content embedded, include practical techniques, life-like simulations (you know, practice), and real-life evangelism opportunities, it's quite easy."

Brandon wasn't buying it. "This is part of my problem: I don't know what to do to get us moving in reaching people on the home front. We're doing great with our missions' programs, but . . ." he trailed off, not sure just how to express his frustration. After a moment he said, "Evangelism programs just seem like word-for-word sales pitches. They are not touching people where they are."

Jerry truly did feel Brandon's pain. He tried to reassure him. "I wasn't sure what we were going to do in Romania either. But once I took the Good Soil Evangelism and Discipleship training and used their resources, I knew we wanted to translate them into Romanian and use them there."

Brandon, surprised by Jerry's answer, retorted, "I know you saw some people trust Christ and develop well in their faith back in New York after your mission board trained you in Good Soil, but what makes you think that Good Soil resources will be universal? Did you drink the Kool-Aid™?"

"Whoa! Listen to the skeptic!" Jerry shot back. "Why so cynical? After all, you are searching—and asking—for help in this area, aren't you?"

Brandon let out a sigh. "I don't know. I guess I'm just tired of people thinking there is a one-size-fits-all program for evangelism."

Jerry agreed, "No problem there. Good Soil would never promote such a thing. In fact, Good Soil is just the opposite. For example, they promote a concept they call *Peeling the Worldview Onion*. This technique helps the evangelist understand where his friends are coming from so he can then share to meet their specific needs.

Peeling onions also serves as an icebreaker and a method to help people feel comfortable. We want to deal with people where they are in life.

"But getting back to your question about Good Soil being universal, I think the concepts and the resources can work pretty much anywhere in the world. In fact, that was one of their objectives: to develop methodology and resources that could work in any culture."

Samson jumped in, "We use Good Soil, too. The training we received and now share with our people does all of what Jerry was sharing: provides Bible-based content, practical how-to techniques with life-like simulations, and real-life opportunities. We even have worldview onion-peeling parties and faith story-sharing parties. We've found Good Soil to be totally transferable. Several of our people now train not only in our own church, but in other churches around Ohio."

"Another thing I think is important in evangelism training is a hand-in-glove type of thing—the training and the resources fit well; they match up," Smitty commented. "Does Good Soil do that well?"

"Very well," Jerry answered. "Once the chronological Bible study philosophy is established, out come the easy-to-use books that help the evangelist/disciple-maker walk through God's Word chronologically. Good Soil's theology of evangelism and their tools fit together perfectly."[6]

Samson added, "The Exchange[7] is another good evangelism resource whose training and tools fit hand-in-glove. Navigators,[8] Cru,[9] and others also provide resources which are consistent with their training. We just use Good Soil because it is more comprehensive, and we believe it provides the Biblical context necessary to help a person deconstruct worldviews and make a solid faith response. The key is getting the training to the people. Many pastors and leaders take Good Soil or other evangelism training with excitement, but some never equip their congregations—transfer doesn't occur."

"Whew," Brandon sighed. "You're hitting the nail on the head. I've taken more seminars than I can count. But I've not gotten transfer in my own life—from my head to my heart and hands—I've just not gotten it done, let alone see it transferred to my people. God help me."

It was a sober moment for the quartet, but powerful. First Samson asked, "Could I pray for you, Brandon? For all of us?" Then the four of them all had the sweetest time of prayer any could remember in a long time.

As they finished, Brandon lifted his head revealing glistening eyes and whispered, "Thanks, guys. I'm beginning to see Jesus' command as the Great Co-Mission—yes, something we all need to do; but something we need to do *together*. I'm also seeing that proper equipping is key to making that happen."

---

6 The Good Soil Integration Model demonstrates their philosophical/theological agreement with methodology. The model is online at: https://www.goodsoil.com/blog/biblically-what-drives-good-soil/

7 https://exchangemessage.org/

8 https://www.navigators.org/

9 https://www.cru.org/

Fun While It Lasted

Bags were packed; the cars were loaded, and the guys were just putting the finishing touches on the house before they took off. As Samson ran the vacuum down the hallway, Brandon and Jerry unloaded the dishwasher, and Smitty finished wiping the table and counters.

Brandon shouted over the vacuum noise, "You guys are going to continue helping me think through and implement the essentials of a truly evangelistic church, aren't you? I'm excited about what I've learned, and I've committed to change in my own life and the life of the church, but I don't want this to just fizzle."

Jerry answered, "Right, like young people and camp decisions."

"You got it," Brandon responded. "That's what I'm afraid of."

Samson put the vacuum cleaner away and stepped into the kitchen as Smitty queried, "So how are we going to do that?"

"Do what?" Samson asked.

"Continue to encourage Brandon—and each other—and develop these essential thingamabobs for an evangelistic church."

Samson replied, "I was thinking about that this morning. There's no reason we couldn't do some study on this individually and meet once a month or so digitally, is there? With all the platforms available these days—Skype, Zoom, Microsoft Teams—we ought to be able to find something all of us are savvy enough to use."

"Yeah," added Smitty. "Even I can use Zoom, as long as one of you calls me. I just click on the invite and I'm in. I feel like I'm a regular techie!"

"Great!" Brandon raved. "How soon can we get together?"

With a Wednesday morning Zoom call planned for 21 days out, bear hugs were shared all around. Then each hopped in their cars, Jerry in his rental, and another annual College Buddy Reunion was in the history books.

Oops, We Forgot Something

"Hey, how's it going, Smitty?" Brandon greeted his buddy through the computer screen. "You're the first one on? Wow, I didn't expect that."

Before Smitty could respond with a funny comeback, Samson's picture popped up with a ding, and then Jerry's.

"Hello."

"Howdy, partners! What's up?"

"You guys ready to talk about essential number 6?" asked Brandon.

"About that," replied Samson. "I'm thinking we might want to rethink this thing."

Concerned, Brandon answered, "What? You don't want to do this anymore?"

"No, no," chuckled Samson. "That's not it at all. I just got to realizing something this past week that would change the order of our essentials. Here's the thing: we thought that training, equipping the saints for the ministry, should be the next thing to concentrate on after:
1. We as pastors are being good shepherds, reaching out to the lost.
2. We gather an E-Team around us.
3. We make sure the Great Commission is THE mission of our churches.
4. We ensure a strong local focus is emphasized.

But I remembered that our church struggled with something a few years back that, once we dealt with it effectively, allowed our evangelistic efforts to thrive which resulted in natural church growth."

"What was that?" Jerry asked.

"Congregational warmth," came the reply.

"Okay," Smitty responded slowly, unsure. "Help us out."

"All right. Here's what happened." Samson took a deep breath and launched into his story. "As we were first training several key people in Good Soil E&D (those we were calling Pew Leadership and what we're referring to now as the E-Team), we were feeling pretty good about ourselves and our outreach efforts. After all, we had eleven people conducting evangelistic Bible studies using *The Story of Hope*—not bad."

"No, that's great!" encouraged Brandon. "I'll take that!"

Samson continued. "Yeah, but at the same time, we were changing sites, going through a 'Pardon our Dust' season with the facility, and each of the pastors were swamped. When the dust settled and we tried to get back to normal, we pulled out the neglected visitor registration cards and found out that in just two months, 57 visitors had come and gone. We only kept one of them—and that was our youth pastor's brother who moved into the area."

"Wow, that's not good," Smitty stated simply.

"No, it's not," agreed Samson. "We determined we would visit every one of those visitors and ask them what they thought of their visit, and if possible, why they didn't come back. Almost all of them said that no one talked with them. I'm sure that a few of our people smiled at these visitors and said, 'Hello,' but the visitors felt that no one cared. I remember that time vividly. Our people were serving and excited about our new facility, but visitors were not feeling it.

"Several issues added to the problem: the parking lot was muddy; the way the construction was going on left people in doubt as to where one should enter the building; we had no signage up to show where the nursery was located or where one should take their kids to class. We hadn't thought that any of those things were a problem, but as we probed and the neglected visitors opened up, we discovered several issues. What an eye-opener for us!"

Happy Visitors

"So, what did you do?" asked Jerry.

"Well, first, we apologized to each of our snubbed visitors and asked them for another chance. Then we initiated PIE."

"Oh, good," Smitty remarked. "Dessert is always helpful."

"I can't disagree with that," Samson chuckled, "but our P in PIE stood for *Prepare the Place and the People*. We looked all over our facilities, inside and out, to see if the place was welcoming. Several of us actually drove in the driveway and walked in the building trying to imagine it was our first time. From that perspective came the following changes we needed to make:

- Parking spaces reserved for visitors closest to the entrances.
- Signs posted in the driveway, the parking lot, and on the building, pointing people to the principal entrances for worship, classes, etc.
- Signs inside indicating where to find the restrooms, nursery, worship center, visitor center. If we could think of something we thought someone would want to find, we made a sign for it.

"*Preparing the People* started with us, the pastors. We decided that no matter how busy we were, no matter how much we had going on any given Sunday, we were going to model friendliness to visitors. Before and after services, even if we only had time to say, 'Hi,' and tell someone we would see them later, we would be sure to greet people with a word and a smile.

"Then, I preached a series on hospitality which we followed up with training. Even though the objective of the hospitality series was to have every member warmly greet visitors and each other, we trained a group of people to be greeters.

"Believe it or not, 18 of those originally shunned visitors are now members of our church and," Samson paused while counting on his fingers, "eight of them are either greeters or on the hospitality committee."

"Cool!" exclaimed Smitty. "But I'm still waiting for P-I-E," he said, dragging out and almost spelling the last word.

"So," responded Samson, eager to continue, "once we figured we had some good systems in place, we wanted to take advantage of them. We encouraged our people to invite friends to what we called Red Carpet events. These are concerts, our Fourth of July fireworks/carnival day, Friend Day, etc. As we plan each year, we try to have no less than eight special, visitor-friendly days. These events are not only for what you might call random visitors; they also create great opportunities for unbelievers involved in evangelistic studies and new believers to assimilate into the church."

Different Strokes

"Okay," interrupted Brandon, "*Prepare the Place* and the *People, Invite*, and . . .?"

"*Embrace*," Samson answered.

"You give your visitors a hug?" Smitty asked incredulously.

"Sure," Samson responded, "it was part of our training!"

Samson's three friends, all with raised eyebrows, were not sure what to say. Samson let his response linger for a moment, and then he roared, "No!" and laughed. "But our training did include teaching our people how to read a new attender's comfort level with personal attention and how they should respond accordingly. We want people to *feel* embraced—to feel comfortable and safe—but that means something different for everyone.

"Some church visitors are shy and are comfortable with little attention. We trained our people to be warm and friendly with these folks, but to give them space. Others want to be engaged in friendly conversation; they even expect it! So, our people are trained to let the visitor lead the conversation, not pressing or trying to go too deep, too quickly. Our objective is to meet all types of visitors where they are and help each one feel embraced, whatever that might mean for them."

Jerry had been silent, listening intently. Now he spoke. "I like that, PIE, *Prepare, Invite, Embrace*, and it's easy to remember. What do you do as a follow-up: to encourage people and let them know they are welcome to return? When we were in seminary, the tradition was that the pastor would make a personal visit to a visitor's home. But I don't see that happening much anymore. Besides, I know many places in Europe, maybe in the States, too, in which it would be inappropriate to visit someone's house unannounced."

"Right," responded Samson, "I think each culture, possibly each community, needs to see what type of action fits best in their context. We make a point to send a note personally signed by me, the senior pastor, after a first visit. Then, if someone returns a second or third time, one of us pastors will make a personal visit—but only after calling or texting first."

"That's good," Jerry replied, "something appropriate must be done. I agree that things have changed, but I think too many churches, scared away from making personal house calls, do nothing to acknowledge visits to their church and therefore lose the opportunity to encourage them to come back."

Sine Qua Non

"True," Brandon murmured softly. "So, what we're saying is that this business of being a friendly church—what'd you call it—congregational warmth? That should be next in our quest of being a truly evangelizing church; it should come *before* training."

"Well, kind of," replied Samson, unsure.

"What's wrong?" Smitty asked.

"Well," Samson answered, "I'm not really sure what we're talking about is a 12-step program or things that must be done in a certain order—one after the other—or it won't work."

"I know, right?" agreed Jerry. "I'm thinking these are essentials—*sine qua non*—things which, if they don't exist, a church probably isn't going to be evangelistic, but they don't have to occur in order. In fact, once a church gets moving on some of these, they should be occurring simultaneously, no?"

"That's what I'm thinking," Samson assured. "There is a sense of priority though, and that's why I'd like to see congregational warmth come before training. Hear me out: if the lead pastor isn't passionately seeking the lost like a good shepherd, a church will have a very difficult time ever becoming a truly evangelistic church, right?"

"Right," the other three responded in unison.

"That's why we put it first. It is a priority," Samson continued. "Then, we the pastors must build a core—an E-Team—that will help motivate and lead the church in evangelism and discipleship."

Everyone was tracking. In fact, Jerry interrupted and carried the baton. "With a passionate pastor and an E-Team in place, they can guide the church in focusing on THE mission of making disciples (three), ensuring that it maintains a local focus (four)."

Brandon grabbed the ball. "That's it. But now, Samson, you're saying that with the direction and focus set, a local church must create a milieu of congregational warmth within which training can take place."

"Right!" Samson encouraged. "If this warmth is not established, the visitors and new people—fruit from the training—will not be received ardently and passionately when they show up at services. Hence, the priority of at least thinking through the importance of developing a warm congregation must happen early on.

"But prioritizing congregational warmth as we have is important for another reason: I was once part of a church in which the mission was to be a warm church! That's not it at all. The mission still needs to be making disciples, but being a warm congregation can help us get there."

"Definitely!" agreed Smitty as the others also affirmed that statement.

Chuckling, Jerry shared his screen with the guys as he said, "All this talk of priorities and milieus got me to thinking about our model." He had

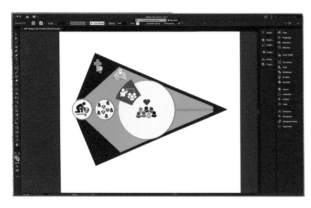

already placed essentials one through four on the screen. He continued, "As you can see, I've put first things first-- passionate, lost-sheep-seeking pastor, then the E-Team. But then, we pull back and make sure the main thing is the main thing: THE Mission," as he placed the cross and globe symbol within a dark blue forward-pointing arrow. "And within that arrow is the Local Focus symbol with its own smaller arrow. Now it looks like to me that we need an environment of congregational warmth within which other essentials might be developed, like equipping, for example." As he finished, he placed a training icon within the congregational warmth circle.

"Hey, that's making sense," complimented Brandon.

Smitty added, "It's looking pretty good, dude."

"Yeah, the model is coming together," encouraged Samson.

Brandon cut the compliments short. "Hey, listen, guys: I've got to get going. I'm meeting with my new pew few tonight at a local Starbucks.™ I've three couples and two singles who I think will make a good E-Team. But hey, if they agree to be my E-Team, I'm going to have to give them some training. I'm going to have to find out about this Good Soil stuff or something. Can someone help me with that?"

Jerry responded quickly, "Yeah, sure. I'll give you a call tomorrow if you like."

"Great, thanks."

"No problem. Talk to you tomorrow."

"See you, guys."

"Later. Greet your wives for me."

Teamwork

Brandon had started out skeptical about Good Soil Evangelism & Discipleship, but since both Jerry and Samson were using it successfully and speaking glowingly of its transferability, he decided to learn more about it. Smitty also wanted to give it a try. Jerry called Brandon the next day as he promised, and since a seminar was scheduled for just a couple of weeks away in October, the two of them decided to go.

After Jerry had taken the training several years back, he put it into practice right away while he was raising up financial and prayer partners. He was a natural trainer, so toward the end of his support-raising stint, Jerry team-taught with a couple of guys from Good Soil in several locations. Once he got to the field, he sponsored the translation of the Good Soil workbook, *The Story of Hope*, *The Way to Joy*, and their respective leader's guides into Romanian. Eventually, he brought together a team of Romanians to train others in that country.

Now, Good Soil asked him to teach at least once while on furlough. So, Jerry was one of the team of three trainers who taught the group of which Brandon and Smitty were a part that October. They loved the interactive training, and since Smitty was planting a church and Brandon had recently seen the need to be involved in personal evangelism and bring church members along on the journey, they both took what they learned and applied it right away.

The friends ended up missing October for the 'meeting every month or so,' which they had agreed upon, but on November 10th, everyone was excited to catch up. However, it was Brandon who was most anxious for the call.

As he entered the call, he noticed the other three were already on. Brandon nearly exploded, "I truly did not expect this! I'm amazed at what God is doing."

"Since I had already determined I would use the Good Soil resources after I got back from the training in Harrisburg, I went ahead and scheduled a training event back here for the end of October before I attended the training. After we trained them here, people immediately began 'peeling worldview onions,' finding friends and family open to the gospel, and we already have several studies being conducted weekly in *The Story of Hope*. It seems too good to be true!"

Samson responded first. "That is amazing. I don't know if I've ever seen a church get so involved so quickly."

"Well, that could go back to our first essential of a truly evangelistic church—a Good Shepherd Pastor," interrupted Smitty. "Since our time together in Erie, Brandon has been making it a priority to have redemptive conversations with unbelievers, and I think his church people have noticed. Since he was modeling for them and then providing training, they are responding."

"Praise the Lord!" cheered Jerry.

"Yes," gushed Brandon. "I've been praising God daily for the way He is working. But listen, as I talk with the people conducting these studies, I see that their friends are hearing and **understanding** God's word, and I anticipate that people will be **embracing** the word soon and will need to be encouraged to **hold fast** to it.[10] I realize this means that our people need to help these new believers through basic first-steps discipleship."

"Right, responded Samson, "Paul tells us we've got to make sure they are rooted and built up in Jesus 'just as we were taught.'[11] But we've got to go slow with baby Christians, starting with what Peter calls milk."[12]

"So," Brandon continued, "I've got copies of *The Way to Joy* and believe the people are prepared to use it. But should this be done one-on-one?"

"Yes," answered Jerry matter-of-factly. "And no," he continued. "Over the years, I've found that the deepest and most permanent impression comes through the personal touch of a one-on-one situation. But there is a place

---

10 Understanding, embracing, and holding fast to God's word are Good Soil principles which come from the parable of the sower recorded in Matthew 13, Mark 4 and Luke 8.

11 "Therefore, as you received Christ Jesus the Lord, so walk in him, rooted and built up in him and established in faith, just as you were taught, abounding in thanksgiving." Colossians 2:6-7

12 "Like newborn infants, long for the pure spiritual milk, that by it you may grow up into salvation—if indeed you have tasted that the Lord is good." 1 Peter 2:2-3

Gaining Ground as a Truly Evangelistic Church

for congregational discipleship, too, in which the local church welcomes new believers into the family and nurtures them to maturity. Discipling in groups helps with assimilation, too, and can provide better stewardship of time and energy over one-on-one settings."

"Yep," agreed Smitty. "In Huntington, we are doing all those things. It may be best to be sensitive to individuals and what is already happening in your environment."

"But you are right, Brandon," Samson encouraged, "Basic discipleship is an essential for a truly evangelistic church, and it probably should be the next one as we think through the process."

"Agreed," added Jerry. "I had a couple of thoughts come to mind as we talked about basic discipleship. One is this: as you disciple individuals, you'll want to be making not only disciples, but also disciple-makers—you'll want to be training them to disciple others as well.

Brandon remarked, "You know, I've always heard that there are four generations in 2 Timothy 2:2—four people or sets of people who 'passed it on': Paul to Timothy to 'faithful men,' to 'others.'"

"Right!"," Jerry replied. "So, we should be able to see this 'passing it on' not only in our lives, but in the lives of our disciples—people we bring to the Lord and develop—as well. They should be passing it on, too!"
"I hope to see that kind of thing in my church," remarked Brandon.

"And there is no reason you won't if you keep at it and trust the Lord to work," encouraged Jerry. "The other thing I wanted to share here is this: people may want you to be their discipler. I know several of us missionaries who had that experience—new believers felt they were getting a second-rate product if the missionary wasn't doing the discipling. They may feel the same about being trained by 'laymen' as opposed to the pastor."

"Yes," Samson added, "we saw something similar, but as we pushed forward and had more and more solid people on our 'Pew Leadership' (what we're calling our E-Team in this group) discipling others, that misunderstanding was dispelled."

Always One More Thing

"This is great! Thanks for the help," Brandon acknowledged. "Listen, before we end the call today, there's something else I was wondering."

"Shoot!" replied Smitty. "I've got a few more minutes. What about you guys?"

"Yep."

"Sure."

"Well, I was wondering . . . I mean, I have gained so much from our times together, and I got to thinking, what about other pastors who may be struggling like I was (and still do!)? They want to be more evangelistic; they want their churches to be, but they're not sure where to start, or they just could use some counsel, or an ear, somebody to listen. Couldn't we form some kind of a . . . I don't know, network of pastors and churches or something through which we could help each other?"

"Ha!" laughed Jerry, maybe a bit too strongly.

"Did he say something funny?" Smitty asked. "Because if he did, I missed it. And I'm always up for a good laugh."

"No, not all! I'm sorry for laughing," Jerry apologized. "Here's the thing: the Good Soil Team always has a debrief time after any training event, and in October we were talking about this very thing. They've noticed that people, especially pastors, seem to love the training, but sometimes seem to have trouble with implementing it in their local churches. These pastors don't seem to know where to start."

"I can relate to that!" exclaimed Brandon.

"Yeah, I've been there," agreed Smitty.

"I think we all have, at one time or another," added Samson.

Jerry continued. "So, the Good Soil Team is adding a pastoral coaching element to their training and resourcing offerings. I think this network idea could fit in nicely with that and could even end up being more productive."

"Hmm," grunted Samson. "I like it. Coaching is great, but this added aspect of iron sharpening iron, sharing, and hearing ideas from other pastors—colleagues in the trenches, so to speak, could be powerful."

"Right?" Jerry added. "But it would have to keep its focus: helping churches to be truly evangelistic. If pastors want help in other areas, they can go somewhere else."

"Well, listen to you!" Smitty exclaimed.

Jerry blushed. "Okay, that sounded a bit . . ." Jerry stopped, searching for the right word.

"Mean?" asked Smitty, giving him a hard time.

"Yes, mean," responded Jerry. "Forgive me," he added dramatically with a flurry of hand gestures and bowing of his head.

"But you know what I mean, right? We would want this network to be simply to help and encourage each other to be evangelistic."

"Yes," Samson jumped in, "and I appreciate the sentiment. We could call it the *ECHO Network—Helping Churches Sound Forth the Gospel*, based on our study of 1 Thessalonians. We would want to help each other be models like the Thessalonica church was."

"I like it!" Jerry exclaimed. "Well, we probably all have to run. I'll talk to my fellow trainers at Good Soil, and we'll pursue this more. So, when is our next meeting?"

Samson spoke first. "Thanksgiving is coming, then Christmas. Can we meet before the end of the year, or should we wait till January?"

Brandon spoke up. "As long as it's early enough in December—before the parties and things start—I'm fine."

"Sure, me, too," agreed Smitty.

"What about December 3rd? Can we carve out a couple of hours that morning?" asked Jerry.

"Okay, sounds good," Samson stated. "See you all at 10:00 on the third. Be thinking about what makes a truly evangelistic church. I think our model is developing nicely. It would make sense for us to share it with people in our future *ECHO Network!*"

"Salut!"

"See you."

"Later."

Keeping It Real

Brandon jumped on the video call with, "I've got it!"

"What have you got?" asked Smitty. "The flu?"

Chuckling, Brandon continued, "Nope. We were supposed to be thinking about what else might be an essential for a truly evangelistic church, and I came up with one: *Peer Accountability.*

"I realized that what made a huge difference for me in staying on task (and the thing Smitty shared back at our retreat that kept him diligent in sharing the gospel), was being kept accountable by someone. We *know* God wants us to evangelize, and we know how important it is for people's eternal futures, but most every one of us needs a loving admonition to step out of our comfort zones and do what we know we should be doing. And I think peer accountability will help keep us on track not only in our evangelism, but also in our discipleship."

"Yes," responded Samson. "This is a very real need which certainly has biblical support. The New Testament is full of encouragement to admonish one another and encourage one another."[13]

Jerry chuckled softly under his breath and then explained. "I remember being in Hong Kong as a missionary apprentice for 7 weeks one summer during college. Five of us students were busy, working hard to meet young people and build a youth group for the missionary and pastor with whom we were working. The church had 30 members, but not one teenager.

"But I noticed one guy on our team seemed to be doing nothing but wander around all day every day. In fact, we all noticed. I talked with this big, tough jock and found out that he didn't have a clue about what to do and was afraid to approach any unbeliever. I determined to spend time with him, do a bit of sightseeing and ease him into it, but make sure we were doing ministry together as well. I got heat from some of the others on the team, but just hanging out with him, allowing some safe time, but keeping him accountable, turned his seven weeks into more of a positive missions experience instead of a colossal flop.

"And now our mission encourages a coach and an accountability partner for our missionaries as they are in the support and partner-raising period of their careers. The coach and accountability partner make sure the missionaries stay on task."

Brandon interrupted, "I hate to admit it, but just knowing that I was going to have to answer Jerry's questions about whether I asked my neighbor to have that Bible study or took advantage of an appointment I had, made a difference in my faithfulness of following through. Am I weak or what?"

Jerry responded quickly, "Nope. You're human. I think that's why God inspired these 'one-anothers' Samson referred to. The writer to the Hebrews tells us to 'consider how to stir up one another to love and good works'— there is no greater love shown or better work done than sharing the gospel; making disciples— '. . . encouraging one another, and all the more as you see the Day drawing near.'[14] We all need the help we can give to one another just by being available and having the courage to ask about how our dear friends are following through on their responsibilities to make disciples."

---

13 Colossians 3:16; 1 Thessalonians 4:18; 5:11; Hebrews 3:13; Hebrews 10:25 are a few of the verses containing the 59 'one-anothers' in the New Testament.

14 Hebrews 10:24-25.

"Perfectly true," Samson replied. "Peer accountability is essential to keeping a church on track to becoming and being truly evangelistic. So how can we encourage this, let's say, in a group or network of pastors?"

"Well," Smitty ventured, "it needs to start with the pastor—the Good Shepherd pastor who goes after lost sheep needs to model this. He needs to have someone who keeps him accountable. Then, as he naturally shares about his experiences whether in sermons, teachings, or one-on-one encounters, people will see that even the pastor needs this type of help and encouragement."

"Exactly!" Brandon nearly shouted. "If it makes a difference for us, our people will see it can make a difference for them."

"So, here's another question," Jerry stated. "Is this something only done one-on-one?"

"That's a great question," acknowledged Samson. "The answer is once again, 'No. And yes.' Peer groups can be helpful, but nothing takes the place of the total honesty which occurs between two people who have agreed to be open with each other and keep themselves accountable. I'm part of a group of five MAPpers—*My Accountability Partners*. I enjoy it, we ask each other questions like, What are you reading? How is God working in your life? In what areas are you struggling? How can I pray for you? How can I better reflect Christ in my work or ministry?

"But it is just not as intimate as meeting with one person and being answerable to that person about your struggles and victories. We really don't open up much on those great topics in a group of five guys.

"With that said, *Worldview Onion Peeling Groups* and similar meetings can be great to encourage each other to keep at these kind of evangelism tasks. For example, when someone who hasn't been peeling onions (asking questions to get to people's core beliefs) sees others being successful at it, they can get excited about doing it, too."

"Right!" responded Jerry. "I remember years ago, going out on what we called *Evangelism in Action*. When we returned from visiting people's homes who had visited our church or who recently had a baby, etc., we would report on what happened. How excited we were when, even though we might have had a not-so-successful visit or had three 'nobody homes,' we heard someone else share how a couple came to Christ during their visit!"

"Amen! So," ventured Brandon, "whether *Peer Accountability* is done one-on-one and/or in groups, we think it is a necessity, it is essential for an evangelistic church."

"Yep, I think we're in agreement," Smitty replied. "You know, what we've been doing here is kind of an accountability group, isn't it?" Everyone nodded and smiled. But before anyone had a chance to say anything, Jerry jumped in, wanting to change the subject.

"Hey, listen, guys, I spoke with the Good Soil Team about the network idea we talked about last time." He paused. "Hmm, another version of peer accountability really . . . Anyway, they're pumped up and ready to begin. From the last training event in October, they've got six churches right now who want to participate. They're actually fine with starting small and building as more pastors and churches see the need to pursue being truly evangelistic. But with those six churches and ours, we'd have ten. They suggested starting on January 15th – giving time to communicate the date with everyone. They'll do all the contacting; all we have to do is show up and participate. What do you say?"

"Yeah, cool!"

"I like it!"

"Uh," answered Samson, checking his calendar, "January 15th looks good. We going to do this through Zoom or in person?"

"They're going to communicate with everyone and see if we can have the first meeting in person."

Still *Keeping It Real*

The first ever meeting of the ECHO Network appeared to be a great success. Sixteen people showed up—9 of the 10 pastors who had expressed interest and seven leaders which some of the pastors brought with them. What a time they had praying together and encouraging one another!

After the Good Soil trainers conducted a fun activity which reviewed Good Soil principles, Samson and Jerry walked through the eight essentials the four friends had been working on, displaying the *Essentials Model* through Power Point. Then, they asked the men, seated four to a table, to discuss the eight essentials in their group before they brainstormed answers to questions they had put up on the screen:

The ECHO Network

- Is that it?
- Are these the essentials of a truly evangelistic church?
- Are there other things that would contribute to a church's pursuit of being truly evangelistic?

The groups were to think through any essentials they had agreed upon and prioritize them before writing them on their flip charts. Interestingly, two groups listed *Prayer*, as their number one essential, while the other two included *Evangelistic Praying* and *Praying for Opportunities* as high priorities.

Samson debriefed the groups.

Pray For Us, Too

"So, tell me Table 1," Samson started out, "Why did you say, *Prayer*? It seems like a good answer, of course, but it's almost like a typical Sunday School answer.

"Well," a young pastor, the spokesman for Table 1 responded, "We just think that we can't expect to do anything worthwhile—let alone evangelism— without a real dependence on God. Prayer demonstrates that dependence."

"Okay, good," Samson thanked the group and moved to the next one. "Now you put down *Evangelistic Praying*. How is that different from what Table 1 shared?"

The table leader from Table 2, a middle-aged pastor replied, "We certainly agree that we cannot do anything without God's blessing, but we see more in this phrase *Evangelistic Praying*. We all expressed how we get discouraged hearing prayer request after prayer request about physical concerns. Now, God wants us to bring those to him, sure, but we're not hearing our people ask for prayer for their unbelieving friends and family. Okay, yes, there are occasions, but they're few and far between. We'd like to see a higher percentage—could we say half—of the prayer requests being, "Pray for so-and-so, my friend, who needs the Lord."

Table Three's rep spoke up. "Related to that, we felt that an evangelistic church would not only be interceding for lost people to come to Christ but asking for opportunities to share the gospel. If we're asking for those opportunities, we are more likely to take advantage of them when they come."

"Also," a tablemate spoke directly to Samson and Jerry, "praying for opportunities is kind of connected to the last essential you shared: when we ask our church friends to pray for opportunities to share with specific friends or family, we are more motivated to share through the peer accountability which arises from asking for prayer."

"Excellent!" encouraged Samson. "So, I think we're all getting this idea that a key essential of a truly evangelistic church would be *Evangelistic Praying*."

The discussion continued for several minutes with Samson writing the main points on the white board. When the discussion wound down, the white board looked like this:

A Truly Evangelistic Church will pray...
1. For Unbelievers to come to Christ and for receptive hearts.
2. For Believers to Share Christ.
    a. For Opportunities
    b. For Boldness
    c. For Clarity
3. For Harvesters.

"That's great," commented Jerry as he stood, and Samson sat. "We need to get going, so I'm going to break a trainer's rule. Normally, a good trainer would not ask a question to be answered directly from the bigger group without allowing for discussion at the table first. But, I'll ask you all to think about the question for a moment and write an answer on one of the 3x5 cards on your table. (That way I can avoid breaking that rule! Whew!) Here's the question: What are some steps we can take to lead our churches in becoming evangelistic pray-ers?"

Jerry wrote the question on the board to allow for contemplation. After just a couple of minutes, Jerry asked for responses.

"We need to model evangelistic praying ourselves; let our congregations hear us practice what we teach."

"Good. Someone else?"

"Maybe we could divide request time into two or more periods—one for physical needs, maybe other requests. But then one period only for evangelistic requests—for the things on the list there on the board."

"Yes, excellent. Another?"

"We talked about accountability groups today. Maybe a serious part of those groups and partnerships could be reserved for prayer—specifically for unbelievers ... and opportunities to share with them ... with boldness ... and clarity." Everyone chuckled because it was obvious this brother was reading from the outline and adding to his contribution as he went.

A gentleman on the left side stood, picked up the microphone at his table, fumbled around with it for a moment, and said, "Why couldn't we teach about these different types of evangelistic praying either in a Sunday School class setting or a sermon or a series of sermons?"

"That's a great idea! Thank you," Jerry encouraged. "Anything else before we wrap it up today?"

After a pause and just when Jerry was about to close, came a final, quiet response: "Yes, I've got one," one of Brandon's invitees answered. He talked haltingly, looking at his card as he spoke. "During these evangelistic prayer times we're promoting in our church meetings, couldn't we encourage members to share *answers* to these prayers? To share what God is doing through us as we pray and seek to be obedient?"

"Yes, indeed," encouraged Jerry. "Wonderful contribution. And, I think, that might just lead into what could be our next essential. Here's what I think we'll do if you're all in agreement. Samson, Brandon, Smitty, and I will collect the work you've done here on the flip charts, collate it, and do a little work on it. Then, next time we get together we can share what we've found and finalize, or at least come closer to settling what the essentials of a truly evangelistic church would be. What do you think?"

Everyone nodded or gave verbal assent, and one of the men closed in prayer. The group stood and talked in pairs and small groups for quite a while. Some set up meetings with others with whom they had never fellowshipped before. With the conversation and interaction among them, no one left until another hour had passed, but when they did, all left encouraged and eager to continue with the network. The four friends collected the flip chart papers and agreed when they would have their next call. The next ECHO Network time was set for the end of March.

Share the Joy

By the time the guys had their Zoom call, Jerry had done quite a bit of ground-laying work. He sorted through the lists the pastors and E-Team members had made at the network meeting, coordinated the ones he thought were the same or similar, and ended up with three more essentials. He then reduced them to two-word phrases as they had done with the other essentials and even had ideas for icons which would fill out the model.

Jerry explained all this at the opening of the call and ended with, "So, the first one (or what we might call the 10th essential) is, are you ready? *Shared Rejoicing.*"

"I like the little guys doing jumping jacks," Smitty joked, "But what exactly is *Shared Rejoicing?*"

"Those little guys are rejoicing. They're praising God. They're excited because someone has come to Christ," Jerry responded. "You see, an evangelistic church ought to be experiencing *and demonstrating* as much or more joy over new believers as we do over graduations, weddings, or even our kids' little league games!"

"Yes, that's good," answered Samson. "The 'Lost things'[15] parables speak strongly to this point. In every one of those parables, the person who finds a sheep, a coin, or a son is not just excited, he or she invites others to share in their excitement. So, how do we incorporate this better into the life of the church?"

"That's where I'm going," nodded Jerry. "Any responses?"

Brandon answered first. "Yeah, I've got an idea. Obviously, we ought to rejoice over people coming to Christ in *big* ways in the *big* group—the congregation. After all, when someone trusts Jesus as Savior it is—wait for it—a *big* deal! But I think shared rejoicing can and should happen even over little steps."

---

15 The Lost Sheep, Lost Coin, and Lost Son parables are found in Luke 15.

"What do you mean?" asked Smitty.

"Well, for example," Brandon answered pausing slightly, "in accountability partner or group meetings, we ought to share and get excited when someone we've been working with and praying for agrees to have a Bible study with us."

"Yeah, yeah," Smitty agreed, "or even if our accountability partners share how someone was 'bumped up the scale'[16] a bit, that is cause for rejoicing!"

"Excellent," Samson commented. "So, first of all, we ought to develop a climate of shared rejoicing in our accountability groups—asking others to rejoice with us when we see God working even in small ways bringing people to Himself."

"And then when someone does trust Christ, there's even more occasion for rejoicing," Jerry added. "In our churches in Romania when someone makes a public profession of faith, that is a big step which warrants celebrating. It's one thing to make a profession to family and friends, but it's a bigger step (more public) when it is done at church. We really delight in those declarations of a changed life."

"As should all of us," Samson encouraged. "That's why the 'finder' in the parables asked others to rejoice with him or her—the lost sheep, coin, and son were found! So, small steps in accountability groups and professions of faith in church definitely are ways we can encourage shared rejoicing. Anything else?"

"What about baptisms?" asked Jerry. "A baptism is an expression of a profession of faith, but I think it is more than that and should encourage shared rejoicing. My missionary friends in Brazil have their baptismal services as special occasions on Saturday—not just as an add-on to a normal service. And they are big celebrations in which each new believer shares his or her faith story, and people applaud them after they share their story and when they come up out of the water. Well, you've never seen anything like that celebration—it lasts all day."

"We baptize on Sundays, and it's not all day, but we do celebrate each person

---

16 "Bumping someone up the scale" is Good Soil language used when we see people moving through human spiritual responses on the Good Soil Evangelism & Discipleship Scale as they draw nearer to repenting and trusting in Christ. Go to https://www.goodsoil.com/about/ to see the GSED Scale.

with thunderous applause and even shouting," added Samson.

"Cool," Jerry smiled as he imagined the scene. "Our colleagues in Ukraine make it an all-day affair as well. They gather at the beach on the Black Sea in the morning, hear faith stories, see the people baptized, and celebrate until evening.

"Our services are similar and are not only times of rejoicing, but of testimony to unbelievers. I remember baptizing 26-year-old Adrian and his wife—19 unbelieving family members from Adrian's family alone (along with church members and others) heard Adrian give his faith story, watched him go under the water and come back up, and observed the church rejoice in unison as Adrian and his wife joined the body. The entire scene spoke volumes to this Orthodox family."

"Wow!" exclaimed Smitty. "What an exciting display of God's saving grace! We haven't been involved in day-long baptismal services or anything that big, but truly evangelistic churches in the States are conducting them as celebrations as well.[17] I can see how making believers' baptism a jubilee-type event or a festival is a key—an essential—for a truly evangelistic church. The excitement generated in these 'lost, now found' events is motivating. I definitely want to work on developing a shared rejoicing atmosphere in our baptismal services as well as in accountability groups and other ministries in our church."

---

17 If you've not been part of something like this, you might check out celebration events which churches post on YouTube. Note how even the time and effort the church puts into videos like these emphasizes the fact that this is a momentous event in the lives of the individual and the life of the church.

Keeping It Simple

"So, I see you did some more collating of the answers given at the first ECHO meeting, Jerry," Smitty said as he got online and saw the charts Jerry had displayed in his living room. "Tell us what we're looking at."

"Well," Jerry answered, "even though a couple months ago Samson said he didn't think we were 'talking about a 12-step program,' it looks like we're going to end up having 12 essentials for a truly evangelistic church. But that's okay. Twelve seems like a big number, and they're not necessarily steps to walk through to achieve success, but each one really is important and makes sense as an essential of a truly evangelistic church."

Jerry continued, "The pastors in our ECHO meeting had some great suggestions, like *Shared Rejoicing* which we worked on last time. All of the other suggestions, varied as they were, could be reduced to these last two: *Strategic Simplicity* and *Relentless Pursuit*. I worked on this one—*Strategic Simplicity*—with my E-Team this month, and Samson worked on *Relentless Pursuit*.

"Without going into detail, I'll just say that some of the great ideas the pastors had were similar but not as encompassing, so they become subpoints of what we consider these last two essentials."

"Right," added Samson. "For example, one pastor wrote, 'A pastor and his people must push past opposition,' while another said, 'We must not get distracted from the mission.' When we talk about *Relentless Pursuit* you'll see that these important points—and others mentioned—contribute to our essential which is much broader."

"Yep," Jerry rejoined. "So, let's talk about *Strategic Simplicity* and what that means. Many of the pastors in our network mentioned that they have 'so much going on,' or they 'run out of steam before they get to the main things,' or their 'people are just so busy nowadays.' You may remember that's what got us started on this back in September: Brandon felt that he 'didn't have time to do evangelism.' What all this amounts to is that less important activities tend to replace the essentials, and evangelism is normally the first to go."

Smitty affirmed, "Remember what old what's-his-name at the college used to say all the time? 'Good activities are enemies of the best.'"

They all laughed, remembering their former professor.

"But how do we handle this?" asked Brandon. "We can't just pull out the proverbial machete and start whacking at ministries!"

"Right," agreed Smitty. "People have their favorite ministries. They'll be upset."

"I'm glad you asked," replied Jerry. "I talked with the pastor of my sending church, revealing what we have been doing during the last six months. I walked him through the model and explained each essential, finishing with *Strategic Simplicity*. He gave me permission to do an experiment with some leaders in our church.

"So, I hashed out what I thought might be good action steps for simplifying ministries in a church, and then during this last month I worked with some people at our sending church who, if I was pastoring this church, might be part of my E-Team—sharp leaders."

Brandon interrupted, "What were your steps?" Jerry showed him the chart below and expanded on each point briefly.

Jerry explained, "It turned out to be more than a great exercise. The conclusions we came to regarding several programs of the church were enthusiastically embraced by the senior pastor. He has determined to lead a committee of deacons and church education leaders through the same exercise. Hopefully, our church can strategically simplify our programming and get back to making the main thing

> **Action Steps to Strategic Simplicity**
> 1. Clearly Explain the Strategy of Simplicity
> 2. Don't Start a New Program or Recurring Activity unless it can Pass the Great Commission 'Litmus Test.'
> 3. Review Existing Programs in Light of New Testament Essentials.
> 4. Where There is Genuine and Significant Mission-Potential, Refine and Refocus.
> 5. If a Program is not Making a Genuine and Significant Contribution to an essential Missional Goal of the Church, it should be Eliminated.

the main thing. I'm excited to see what comes out of all this!"

Samson responded, "That's great! Maybe you'll be able to trim out some 'puddle ministries.'"

"Puddle ministries?" asked Brandon. "What are puddle ministries?"

"Well," replied Samson, "if we think of the ministry of the church as a flowing river, headed somewhere, we will want all our ministries to be in line with that direction, flowing along with the river. Puddle ministries are those ministries that aren't part of the river, but that may have somehow even gotten sidetracked from their original purpose or are no longer relevant. People who are involved in puddle ministries aren't headed downriver but are splashing around in a puddle. They may be making a lot of noise, but they're not heading anywhere. Ministries that may have been vital in the past can become puddle ministries. That's why constant evaluation is necessary."

"So," Brandon started hesitantly, "everything is up for grabs?"

"Sure," replied Jerry. "We don't want to go around willy-nilly cutting out ministries, but we do want to evaluate everything, making sure that ministries are in line with the purpose of the church and are not distracting us from our principle objective of making disciples—reaching into the community, evangelizing, and developing followers of Christ."

Samson asked for their attention, "Hey, listen. Two questions before I take off. Can you three attend an ECHO Network meeting on the 10th of next month?" Samson waited as they checked their calendars, and each gave a positive response.

"Great," he continued. "Can we hold off to cover the last essential until that meeting?"

"Yeah." "Sure." "Why not?" came the responses.

"Good. I'll prepare some activity or activities to present *Relentless Pursuit*. If I need your help, I'll let you know during the next couple weeks. Thanks, guys. Gotta go. See you later."

"Ciao for now."

Don't Quit

Samson and his administrative assistant sent emails and made phone calls to the ECHO Network members, and several others they thought might want to consider taking part. The general consensus from the last meeting was that those who could get to the site—wherever they planned to have that particular meeting—in less than a two-hour drive would meet in person while the others joined online. On the 10th of the next month, as planned, they had 8 show up online while 15 gathered at Samson's church building in Cleveland.

After opening in prayer, Jerry led the group in talking briefly about the purpose of the network (for those who were attending for the first time) and then reviewed the essentials succinctly before spending some time on *Strategic Simplicity*. After discussing it, all agreed about the importance of prioritizing ministries to keep evangelism and discipleship as the main mission of the church. Then Samson stepped to the plate.

"So, we've got these 11 essentials," Samson started, waving his arm at the screen displaying the nearly completed model. "But if I were to ask you which of these essentials is most important, what would you say?" He didn't wait for an answer.

"We might say the first one because the pastor is key; he must model and lead the church in evangelism. We might say, 'THE Mission,' because if we get off track from the mission, we've lost our way and won't get the job done. Really, we could make a case for just about any of these because what we are saying is that they—all of them—are essential to be a *truly* evangelistic church. And so, let's leave it at that. These are all essentials—what pastor and people **must** do to be a truly evangelistic church.

"But in keeping with the idea that they are all essential and, therefore, all just as important, I believe there is one more essential: *Relentless Pursuit*. We must develop a dogged determination to keep at it; to not let obstacles keep us from our objective of reaching lost sheep around us and making disciples out of them. And there *will* be obstacles.

"Last time we were together, you guys wrote ideas for essentials on sticky notes. Many of you wrote either the exact same idea or something very similar and those ideas provided us with a list of obstacles. For example, one of you wrote, "We mustn't let discouragement stop us," and another wrote, 'A pastor and his people must push past opposition,' while another said, 'We must not get distracted from the mission.'

"If we take all of these together and other ones that were mentioned, I believe we have our final essential: *Relentless Pursuit*. Here are five hindrances you pastors gave us which we think are common obstacles." Samson clicked the remote and the five obstacles showed up on the screen in front of them.

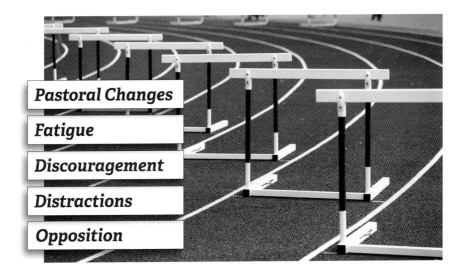

Pastoral Changes

Fatigue

Discouragement

Distractions

Opposition

"Now, just for a few moments, let's concentrate on *Opposition*. What do you think are types of opposition to evangelism which your church either faces now, you've seen in the past, or you anticipate could occur?"

"Political correctness!" Pastor Morse seated in the front shouted. "I frequently run into people who ask, 'How can you preach Jesus is the only way? You shouldn't offend people.'"

"Okay, good," Samson replied. "Well, it's not good that this happens, but that's a good *answer*. Someone else."

From the back a pastor responded, "I've found people are offended and oppose the use of certain terms like, 'conversion' and even 'evangelism.'"

"Right," affirmed Samson, "that kind of opposition can create problems."

"Speaking of offense," an elderly pastor attending virtually spoke up, "I've found that some subjects have become off-limits for sermon topics. I don't know if people don't want to hear about hell or pastors don't want to preach about it, but it's not being preached about as it used to be."

Samson responded, "I've noticed the same thing. You know, that could be considered being politically correct, too—not preaching on subjects that could be offensive." Turning to Jerry in the front row, he continued, "Does any of this sound familiar? We talked about some of this a few months back when you mentioned the Thessalonian church, didn't we?"

"That's right," Jerry responded, jumping up to address the group. "I had shared with my friends a while back how when we have been back in the States for furloughs, we seemed to notice a lack of evangelistic fervor in our supporting churches. We wondered why that was.

"Since then, we've discovered that some people are afraid to share because of not knowing what to say, others because of a fear of rejection, and others because they are afraid of imposing their beliefs on people. I believe that last fear is a form of political correctness which comes from living in a growing pluralistic society. People are intimidated by pluralism by the increasingly common notion in the States that all faith-paths lead to God. People are afraid to speak out for Christ for fear that others will be offended, consider them rude and boorish, or even out-and-out wrong for doing so. After all, 'we would be intolerant to challenge someone else's worldview, wouldn't we?' I even had someone challenge me in one of our supporting churches, asking how I had 'the audacity to seek to convert people' in Romania where 'they have their own religion.' I believe this kind of attitude is keeping people from sharing the gospel with their neighbors."

"Wow," one of the pastors exclaimed. "I've noticed this kind of sentiment growing, but so strong even in an evangelical church... that's hard to take. Although advocates of pluralism will verbally espouse 'tolerance,' pluralists are *intolerant* of churches that preach 'Jesus is *the* Way, *the* Truth, and *the* Life.' And it is espoused so much in the world by seemingly good people, that the church begins to buy into the philosophy."

"Exactly," responded Jerry. "Consequently, any church that preaches that Jesus is the only way will inevitably face persecution—somewhere on a scale between subtle and violent. It's happening already, but it seems we must brace ourselves as the worst is yet to come."

"It is amazing," another pastor agreed. "Seems there's never been a time like the days in which we're living."

"That's just it," Jerry shot back. "It's appalling the mindset believers are adapting from the world, even frightening, but it's not the first time the world has had this perspective." Stepping forward and grabbing his Bible from the chair, Jerry continued. "Before we left for furlough, I wanted to renew a passion in our people for sharing their faith. So, I went to I Thessalonians 1 because I've always been impressed with the way those people came to Christ in a difficult situation and others came to know about their conversion."

Samson had a knowing twinkle in his eye as he added, "And boy, did they let others know about it! It echoed across the region."

"You remember," Jerry smiled. "Acts 17 tells us that when Paul proclaimed Jesus as the Messiah in the Thessalonian synagogue, some Jews and many 'God-fearing Greeks' believed and joined him (verse 4). Verse five says that the Jews 'moved by envy,' recruited wicked men, formed a mob, and created a riot. Not only did the Jews resent losing the Gentiles who had been attending synagogue, I'm sure they also were hoping they would get more proselytes of the Gentiles who had not been in attendance.

"But, how pluralistic was Thessalonica at that time? Well, many were worshiping the Roman gods, Zeus, Heracles, the Dioscuri, Apollo, and Aphrodite. Evidence also exists that the Egyptian gods Isis, Serapis, and Osiris were being worshiped. That's not to mention the cults of Dionysus and Cabirus who had followers in the city nor the civic cults Luke refers to in Acts 17:7."

Smitty interrupted, "Where did you get all this information?"

Jerry replied matter-of-factly, "When I was preparing to preach on 1 Thessalonians, I read several articles.[18] But the point is, Thessalonica was a very pluralistic society. They certainly didn't need to ask themselves, 'Might we suffer persecution if we believe in Jesus the Messiah and stand for Him?' They saw it happen to Paul and the others who brought them the message!"

---

18 Gieschen, Charles, Christian Identity in Pagan Thessalonica: The Imitation of Paul's Cruciform Life, CTQ 72 (2008): 3-5.

"Right," interjected Samson, "Mobs, mayhem, and malice—not only against Paul and the missionaries, but against the people of the town early on. Jason and other believers were dragged before the authorities."[19]

"But in the midst of this pluralistic culture hostile to biblical Christianity, what happened?" Jerry continued. "The life-changing power of the gospel coupled with the power of the Holy Spirit convicted sinners to turn away from idols and to the living God."[20]

"Amen!" interrupted Samson again. "How exciting to see the change in these people. And the order here is important, they placed their faith in God and turned from idols. It was their belief in ONE true living God that caused them to give up their many gods of wood and stone.

"But it was more than a generic faith in God, because even the demons and many non-Christians believe in God. They had faith (from-the-heart belief) in God who raised Jesus from the dead, the Son of God who delivers us from the wrath to come. It was a from-the-heart faith response that was strong enough to cause them to repent."

Pastor Morse, who had spoken up first, had been listening intently, but silent for some time. He commented, "Confusion about repentance abounds among Christians today. The idea that a sinner must repent—and give up his sins—before he or she can come to God in faith is so common. Some Christians, even evangelicals, along with Catholics, Orthodox, and High-Church Lutherans, equate repentance with penance, an act of making amends for past sins by self-abasement or other acts of self-denial."

"You're right," affirmed Samson, "but biblical repentance is simply a 'turning from.' One old-time missiologist called it a 'U-turn of the mind.' So, in this case, the polytheistic idol-worshiping Thessalonians repented of their adherence to idolatry which included rejecting the beliefs and practices that accompanied pagan idol worship. They turned **from** virtually everything they had been taught and believed all their lives and **to** the living God!"

---

19 Acts 17:5-9.

20 "Our gospel came to you not only in word, but also in power and in the Holy Spirit and with full conviction...You turned to God from idols to serve the living and true God, and to wait for his Son from heaven, whom he raised from the dead, Jesus who delivers us from the wrath to come." 1 Thess. 1:5, 9-10.

Gaining Ground as a Truly Evangelistic Church

"And that's why Paul says they were a model for all the other believers and churches in the region,"[21] Jerry jumped into the conversation again. "Now, the 'you' here is collective. They, as a church, modeled what kind of church Paul expected other churches to become. The English word 'model' or 'example' is translated from the Greek word *tupos*, which literally meant to 'strike repeatedly,' in the sense of molding an image, pattern, or form which would be followed in making other images. Others (including us) were to pattern their lives after these Thessalonian believers. We might even think of the 'strikes on the anvil' as the persecutions they suffered at the hands of their pluralistic and polytheistic colleagues because of their new-found faith in the One true living God."

By now every pastor in the room had opened his Bible too, appreciative of the obvious exegesis these men had done. They were seeing that courage in the midst of a pluralistic society was not a new thing! One pastor, still looking down at his Bible, jumped up and said, "But even the monotheistic Jews got in on the action. It was they who formed the mob we read about in Acts 17, but they also would not have been happy with what Paul says in I Thessalonians 1:9. Sure, the Thessalonians 'turned to God from idols to serve the living and true God,' but the core of their newfound Christian faith was that God 'raised [Jesus] from the dead.' This was fuel for more persecution."

"That's right," answered Jerry, "and even though these harsh repeated blows from Jews and polytheists were meant for harm and punishment, they produced an opposite effect. A model church was formed, a pattern for other Christian congregations all over the Roman world, and for us today."

"But what did they model?" asked Smitty. "What specifically is it that we should follow in their example?"

It was Samson's turn to answer, but the next several answers came rapid fire from both him and Jerry, the two who had studied the passage most recently. "They modeled a responsiveness to the Word of God."

"They modeled a ministry of faith and a labor of love."

"They modeled a steadfastness of hope in the Lord Jesus Christ, in spite of 'much affliction.'"

---

21 "And so you became a model to all the believers in Macedonia and Achaia." 1 Thessalonians 1:7 (NIV)

"They modeled a congregational life of Holy Spirit-sourced joy while living in the midst of a pluralistic society that opposed and attempted to suppress every core essential tenant of Biblical Christianity."

"And even though the passage doesn't specifically say it, they undoubtedly were models in sharing their faith with their pagan and Jewish friends."

Jerry wrapped it up with, "And as we shared earlier, they also modeled how to imitate a pastor who imitates Jesus Christ. Verse six says, 'and you became imitators of us and of the Lord.' A great way to become a Christian model, or pattern for others to emulate is to imitate a godly mentor-model yourself. The Thessalonian Christians mimicked what they saw in Pastor Paul's life."

"True!" responded Samson, chuckling. "Pluralists may argue with the content of your Christian faith, but they can't argue with the power of the gospel. Where lives are being changed, they take notice. And their appetites for something real and meaningful in life will be whetted. That's what happened nearly 2,000 years ago in the Roman world, and it can happen today."

"That's right," added Jerry. "In Greece where the majority of people were worshiping gods like Zeus, Hera, Artemis, Apollo, Aphrodite, Athena—a whole slew of them—they were hearing about people who used to worship the same gods, but not anymore. It's quite possible that the Via Egnatia, or Egnatian Highway, which went from Istanbul in the east to Apollonia in the west and passed right through Thessalonica, was the avenue which allowed the news to spread so rapidly."

"Good point, Jerry," applauded Samson. "Look at the verb in verse eight: 'the word *sounded forth* from you.' The underlying Greek word is *échos* from which we get the word *echo*. It is used to express LOUD, reverberating sounds, that *echo* for long distances. And in this case, it was the POWER of the gospel that created that sound. And as Samson said, the Egnatian Highway could have contributed to that echoing."

Pastor Morse added enthusiastically, "You know, atheism, agnosticism, non-Christian religions, even liberal Christianity of our day are all leaving a spiritual void in the lives of people today just as the worship of false gods did in the hearts of Ancient Greeks. Like Paul, I want to be a pastor my people can imitate. I want to see changed lives which can be patterns for others and which 'sound forth' the word of the Lord. I want my church to create a gospel echo, a loud reverberating echo in our community."

"Amen," Jerry concurred. "We all want—well, we all should want that. I'm confident that if lives are being changed in our churches, it will echo, even in a pluralistic world. Guaranteed!"

"Yes, that's true. Now, we talked a long time on pluralism as political correctness. Did anyone else want to mention any other obstacles to evangelism?" Samson asked.

After a long silence, one of Brandon's people spoke up. "Church members are more concerned about being comfortable, keeping things going as they like them rather than seeking to see changed hearts and lives. Some don't like having to sit next to people they don't know and who might be different from them."

"Okay, thanks," Samson acknowledged. "Let's get that up on the board, too."

Samson had been writing one and two word answers on the whiteboard as they were given. His list included:

- Pluralism
- Sermon subjects off limits (e.g. Hell)
- Offensive Terms
- Status Quo/Comfort

"We've got several here, and there may be more, but let's stop for now. Some of these obstacles come from within the church and some from without. Also, we talked about how several of these could fit under a heading called *political correctness*. Now, I'd like to talk about what we can do to climb over, tunnel under, or fight through these obstacles."

The rousing discussion that ensued dealt with antagonistic church members, secular organizations mounting protests, and seemingly everything in between. In the end, below the four prevalent oppositions on the whiteboard, Samson wrote the pastors' conclusions:

- A TRULY evangelistic church must determine that their focus be on those they want to REACH as opposed to those they would like to KEEP.

- Jesus must be our example. He was always concerned with reaching the lost.

"Now, gentlemen," Samson said, moving into conclusion mode, "you see what we did here, right? We dealt with one of the typical obstacles to developing and maintaining a truly evangelistic church: opposition. You all volunteered what you thought were obstacles. We listed them and then we discussed how a church seeking to be truly evangelistic might overcome the barriers. And here is our work.

"I would encourage each of you (I know I am going to do this) to go back to your E-Teams and do something similar with these other obstacles—distractions, discouragement, fatigue, and pastoral changes." Holding up a copy of *Gaining Ground as a Truly Evangelistic Church*, he continued, "For a reference on these topics, you can go to Essential 12 on page 177. The Leader's Guide to the book gives great ideas for interacting with your E-Team. Be sure to take advantage of these tools.

"In Essential 12, it mentions that less than half of the starters of a Spartan race finish the race. Their designation is 'DNF'—Did Not Finish. I don't want to see our churches fall into that category. I am so excited to be part of this ECHO Network because I think we can challenge and encourage one another to overcome obstacles and be finishers. We can help each other to be relentless in our pursuit of being *truly* evangelistic churches."

Thoughts from the Good Soil Team

Even from their college days, Brandon, Smitty, Samson, and Jerry knew the value of networking and partnering. Their kinship continued strong over the years and by God's grace contributed to their fruit in ministry. Expanding that affinity to their colleagues in the ECHO Network would only enhance what they started years ago.

Friend, we invite you to consider becoming part of the ECHO Network too, but more on that later. For now, read through the essentials of a truly evangelistic church which the guys uncovered.

The Essentials

Only Evangelical **or** TRULY Evangelistic?

Leading Your Church to Be TRULY Evangelistic, Not Just Evangelical

Both words, evangelical and evangelistic, are rooted in the Greek word εὐαγγέλιον (euangelion), which means "good news" or "gospel." Although a bit simplistic, an essentially correct distinction is:

- An evangelical church is a church that believes the basic truths of the Biblical gospel.

- An evangelistic church is a congregation that not only believes the gospel, but also strives hard to obey our Lord's command to both broadly proclaim and share it person-to-person with unbelievers.

Is your church only evangelical, or is it TRULY evangelistic?

Please do not misunderstand. To be a *truly* evangelistic church does not mean it should be a *totally* evangelistic church. Evangelism is not the only activity in which a "New Testament" local church should be engaged. But it is probably the most neglected, particularly in this North American generation. So, that is the focus of this book.

With that in mind, let us start with some questions to help you answer the question, "Is my church only evangelical, or is it *truly* evangelistic?" Please read each question thoughtfully and answer frankly, to yourself.

☐ Is the pastor a Luke 15 "Good-Shepherd pastor" who leads the church in evangelism by modeling a lifestyle of pursuing lost sheep with the gospel, in an effort to rescue them from sin and eternal separation from God?

☐ Is there at least a core group of members in the congregation who, like the pastor, are passionate about sharing the good news of salvation with their unbelieving friends, neighbors, and loved ones, as well as others that God brings into their lives?

☐ Does the church have a clearly-defined mission statement—based on the GREAT Commission—that the congregation knows well and is persistently and passionately led to pursue?

☐ Is the church effectively reaching its local community with the gospel, and frequently seeing lives changed, including unbelievers from ethnic groups who are different from the majority ethnicity of the congregation?

☐ Does the congregation feel comfortably warm to visitors who attend the church, even visitors with a variety of personalities? Once they visit, do they want to visit again?

☐ Have members of the congregation been adequately trained (and recently retrained) to develop redemptive relationships with non-Christians and share the gospel clearly and inoffensively?

☐ Do new believers in the church receive the personal guidance and instruction they need to grow in their faith and become mature, reproducing followers of Jesus?

☐ Does the emphasis of evangelism in the church engender a sense of intra-congregational accountability—the sense that we all, "you and I," have a Christian responsibility to tell people about Jesus?

☐ In congregational or small group prayer sessions, is there a healthy percentage of evangelistic prayer requests—prayer requests for unbelievers and for gospel-sharing opportunities?

☐ Is there a genuine sense of excitement and celebration, when the congregation is informed that another "lost sheep has been found," or even when there has been some small but positive response to an evangelistic effort?

☐ Is the church program light enough that church members can expend sufficient time and energy on ministry-related activities that are genuinely THE Mission-driven?

☐ When the congregation is faced with diversions and discouragements that would tend to derail it from its focus on evangelism and discipleship, does it have the commitment to overcome the obstacles and stay the course until Jesus comes?

You probably drive a four- or six-cylinder car or have one of both like I do. I am regularly amazed at the power difference I feel when I switch from driving my four-cylinder to the six. But do you realize that there are 12-cylinder cars out there on the road? Can you imagine what it would feel like to drive a 12-cylinder Lamborghini, Ferrari, BMW, Bentley, Mercedes, or Rolls-Royce? Wow, that's power!

The gospel is the power of God unto salvation—the power that causes personal lives to be changed and churches to grow in the healthiest way, the way Jesus wants to see churches grow. Evangelism is simply a matter of disseminating the gospel so that God can release gospel-power in the lives of unbelievers. Every evangelical church probably does something gospel-related, but many are sputtering along on just a cylinder or two when they could do much better if they (1) knew specifically what to do, (2) knew how to do it, and (3) were committed to seeing their churches become *truly* evangelistic—or, in other words, driving on all cylinders.

Our Evangelism ESSENTIALS Model for Local Churches was designed to help you know specifically what to do, how to do it, and hopefully become a twelve-cylinder church.

The Evangelism ESSENTIALS Model for Local Churches

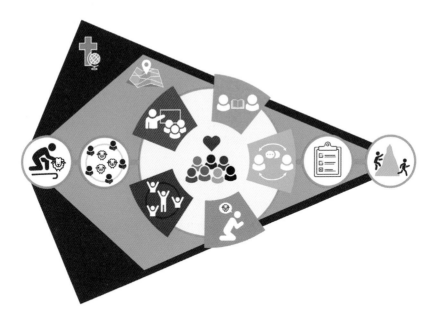

Some pastors and church members might say: "Oh yes, our church is 'evangelistic.' It even says so on our church sign." "We have an outreach team." "Our pastor preaches evangelistic sermons and gives a public invitation in each service." "We have a gospel tract rack by each exit door."

While those things may be good, the foolproof marks of a *truly* evangelistic church are not the words on a church sign, outreach teams, evangelistic preaching with public invitations, or gospel tract racks.

The *true* heart and soul of an evangelistic church is a congregation that is regularly engaged in developing caring "redemptive relationships" that may lead to conversion discussions and personal gospel conversations— conversations that help unbelievers *clearly understand* the gospel and *sincerely embrace* Jesus as Savior.

That may seem impossible to many pastors, but it *is* what our Lord desires for local churches. And we believe it is attainable, if the church's leadership will strive to incorporate these essentials into the core life of the church:

 Evangelistic Pastor: The pastor MUST model, lead, and drive the ministry of evangelism. It is too important to ignore or to delegate to an associate. Period. Exclamation point!

The E-Team: Some leadership from members of the congregation is important—no, it's essential. To identify and mobilize this core group is the pastor's task.

 THE Mission: The church's mission must *truly* be the Great Commission. Just using the "Great Commission" as a pious platitude is not enough.

 Local Focus: A local church cannot jump over the "Jerusalem" of Acts 1:8 and salve its congregational conscience by only supporting foreign missions. A church's first and foremost responsibility is to "bloom where it was planted."

 Congregational Warmth: Most churches need to "warm up" the congregation—especially its friendliness and acceptance of visitors. This will begin to happen automatically the more your congregation becomes involved in personal redemptive relationships, but there are changes that can be made to initiate and accelerate the process.

 Equipped Congregation: Church members must be equipped with worldview-relevant training and resources to become engaged in redemptive relationships that effectively lead to gospel-sharing opportunities. The lack of training or outdated training produces little or no evangelistic outreach.

 Basic Discipleship: In conjunction with evangelism training and resourcing, church members must be equipped for personal discipleship, especially leading new believers in the first steps of their new-found Christian lives. The goal is not just to make disciples, but to make disciples-who-make-disciples, ad infinitum.

 Peer Accountability: A congregational climate of mutual accountability for every-member evangelism must be created. This accountability climate, like leaven, will grow and spread over time if nurtured by the pastor, other leaders, and a core of the congregation's membership.

 Evangelistic Praying: The church needs to focus much of its congregational prayer time on evangelistic contacts. The congregation will need to be led to pray regularly for that which is most important—for what is eternally important: the souls of lost men, women, and children.

Shared Rejoicing: Churches rejoice in the things they most value. When a congregation genuinely rejoices over lost sheep who are found, believers are motivated to seek other lost sheep.

 Strategic Simplicity: Church programming must be simplified by trimming and minimizing official church activities that do not genuinely contribute to the "making disciples and teaching them to observe all things" that our Lord commanded. Caution: Handle with care. This will be a challenge if your church is steeped in history and tradition.

 Relentless Pursuit: The pastor and other church leaders must be determined to stick with these efforts for the long haul. It may take years for some churches to experience significant change. Do not become discouraged and say, "It doesn't work in my church." It's Biblical, it can work anywhere if the first essential (see above) is in place.

Even a 12-cylinder car will not reach its power potential if it is missing on one or more cylinders. Consequently, all gospel-believing and gospel-preaching churches could probably use a tune-up to optimize their evangelistic-power potential. In the twelve chapters to follow, each of these ESSENTIALS will be fleshed out with thought-provoking questions and content, as well as starter ideas for tuning up your church.

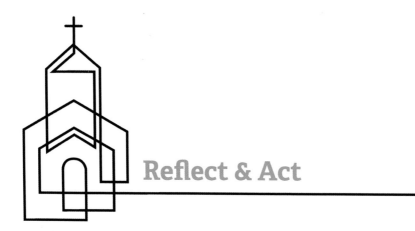

Reflect & Act

Reflect:

1. What is the difference between an evangelical and an evangelistic church?

2. To which of the evaluating questions (on pages 80-82) could you answer *yes* most confidently? Which were most challenging?

3. On how many cylinders do you believe your church is firing when it comes to evangelism?

Act:

1. Begin to pray daily for your church to become truly evangelistic.

2. Go back and match each two-word ESSENTIAL with the icon that represents it on the model on page 83.

3. Share these essentials with at least one other person who you think is also interested in your church being truly evangelistic.

Essential 1
Evangelistic Pastor

Leading by Good-Shepherd Modeling

If the **lead shepherd** ***of the church is not a*** **Good-Shepherd** ***pastor, the*** **congregation will do as he does and ignore the lost sheep all around them.**

Many of us who are Christ-followers know that the New Testament word translated *"pastor" (ποιμήν)* literally means *"shepherd."* So it is entirely appropriate to use these two words interchangeably. And we rightly understand that it is the duty of the pastor/shepherd to "care for his sheep."

But Alford Usher Soord, the famous 19th Century British painter powerfully depicted another essential responsibility of a "Good Shepherd/ Pastor."

Look at—and reflect on—Soord's most famous painting, *The Parable of the Lost Sheep*, and think about what Jesus considers to be true of a good pastor.

Rarely, if ever, will you find a truly evangelistic church that is led in evangelism from the so-called "lay" level up, or even from an associate staff level up.

> [1] Now the tax collectors and sinners were all drawing near to hear him. [2] And the Pharisees and the scribes grumbled, saying, "This man receives sinners and eats with them."
>
> [3] So he told them this parable: [4] "What man of you, having a hundred sheep, if he has lost one of them, does not leave the ninety-nine in the open country, and go after the one that is lost, until he finds it? [5] And when he has found it, he lays it on his shoulders, rejoicing. [6] And when he comes home, he calls together his friends and his neighbors, saying to them, 'Rejoice with me, for I have found my sheep that was lost.' [7] Just so, I tell you, there will be more joy in heaven over one sinner who repents than over ninety-nine righteous persons who need no repentance."
>
> Luke 15: 1-7

Here are some scenarios I have seen all too often: The pastor realizes that his church is failing in its evangelistic outreach, so he convinces the church to hire a Minister of Evangelism and Discipleship to solve the problem. Or the pastor organizes an Outreach Committee and assigns the task of leading the church in evangelism to the committee. Or the pastor sends his staff to an evangelism training seminar but doesn't attend with them. Or maybe the pastor preaches a series of sermons on the Christian's responsibility to share the gospel with unbelievers but does not practice what he preaches.

Churches that are fruitfully reaching their communities with the Gospel of Jesus Christ are doing so because they have a pastor who consistently and persistently 1. **models** personal evangelism in his own life, 2. **leads** his flock to emulate his example, and, as needed, 3. **drives** the evangelistic mission of the church through lethargy and other inevitable kinds of resistance.

A Good-Shepherd Pastor Models Personal Evangelism
By far, the most crucial variable in developing a *truly* evangelistic church is a pastor who consistently goes after lost sheep, leading his own flock by example.

More than 350 years ago, John Selden, a famous English legal expert stated,

"Preachers say, 'Do as I say, not as I do.'" Unfortunately, that is sometimes still true. But the Apostle Paul challenged the Corinthian believers to think and act differently:

> 36 Imitate me, just as I also imitate Christ.
>
> 1 Corinthians 11:1 (NKJV)

The only church that Paul calls a "model church" became a *model* congregation by first becoming an *imitator* of its pastor.

> 6 You became imitators of us and of the Lord, for you welcomed the message in the midst of severe suffering with the joy given by the Holy Spirit.
>
> 7 And so you became a model to all the believers in Macedonia and Achaia.
>
> 1 Thessalonians 1:6-7 (NIV)

Pastor, when it comes to evangelism, how *truly* evangelistic would your congregation be if it imitated you? How many redemptive relationships would your church members be building if they followed your example? How many personal gospel presentations would they be sharing if they emulated your life among unbelievers?

I am reminded of a pastor who reluctantly attended a Good Soil Evangelism and Discipleship Seminar. After decades as a pastor, he admitted: "I have always struggled with evangelism." But in that seminar he learned about "bumping people up the Good Soil scale," "developing redemptive relationships that may lead to conversion discussions," penetrating "worldview noise" that may prevent clear gospel communication, "peeling worldview onions," and using *The Story of Hope* and the *Chronological Bridge to Life* to help unbelievers clearly understand and embrace the gospel.

This pastor went back to his church and began practicing what he learned in the Good Soil Seminar. He conveniently interwove stories of some of his evangelism experiences into his sermons, and his newfound passion gradually began to spread. Soon, others in the congregation began "doing as he did," not just as he was telling them to do. Before long, many of the church's members were sharing the gospel with friends, neighbors, and unsaved loved ones.

One of the three appearances in the New Testament of the word "evangelist" is found in the Apostle Paul's job description for a pastor:

> [4] As for you, always be sober-minded, endure suffering, do the work of an evangelist, fulfill your ministry.
> 2 Timothy 4:5

Who knows—perhaps Timothy was not gifted as an evangelist. Maybe sharing the gospel with unbelievers did not come as easy to him as it did to Peter or Paul or Stephen the deacon. He may have been more gifted in teaching the Scriptures to believers and exhorting them or showing mercy to the needy or the administration of the church's ministry. Whatever the reason, Paul reminded Timothy that pastoral ministry includes "doing the work of an evangelist," specially gifted or not.

Pastors, it's a basic part of your job description.

A Good-Shepherd Pastor Leads His Congregation in Evangelism
In addition to modeling personal evangelism, the pastor mentioned above began leading his congregation to do as he was doing. He began by organizing a Good Soil Evangelism and Discipleship training seminar to be conducted in his church.

Modeling creates the spark, but it takes some leadership to fan the flames. To implement the next eleven "ESSENTIALS for a *truly* evangelistic church" will require leadership from the pulpit.

Initially, at least, this task is too crucial for the pastor to delegate to anyone else. After many years in ministry, I fully understand that pastors are expected to do lots of things—make hospital visits, preside at weddings and funerals, counsel people with complex problems, oversee the church's business affairs, preach interesting and relevant Biblical sermons, and on and on and on. Although all of these are important, they sometimes become an excuse for not being a good shepherd who demonstrates a concern for the lost sheep.

Pastor, if you are going to delegate anything, delegate some of your tasks that prohibit you from developing redemptive relationships with unbelievers and from taking the lead in equipping your congregations to imitate your example. As your church matures evangelistically and you have trained someone to take the lead, you may eventually be able to lead from behind, but you cannot start that way. And you should never relinquish evangelistic leadership entirely.

Evangelistic momentum will only be built by the pastor's leadership. So, as you read the next eleven articles, pastor, see yourself in the role of leading the way in each of these essential congregational culture-changing tasks.

A Good-Shepherd Pastor Drives the Push Through Resistance to Evangelistic Efforts

The word "drive" in this context may conjure up unintended images. Please understand, I'm not suggesting "driving" to be a harsh, negative, and nagging, harping and haranguing kind of activity. I'm simply saying that when the church's evangelistic efforts get mired down because of apathy or diverting distractions from the mission of seeking lost sheep, the pastor must remain positive and lead the push through the resistance. Think of "stuckness" and the needed push or pull or nudge to get "unstuck."

Evangelistic resistance is inevitable. For example, building programs may tend to sap the evangelistic energy of the church. Some kind of crisis in the congregation may divert the church from its pursuit of "*the* mission." As some pastors know by experience, not every member will be happy about the church's efforts to turn a major focus of the church outward. Resistance can be serious if the disgruntled member (or members) happens to be vocal and combative—especially if he or she holds a significant position of leadership in the church. If it is any consolation, remember that this is the kind of resistance the Pharisees brought to the ministry of Jesus.

To quote a famous American frontier hero: "Be sure you are right, then go ahead" (Davy Crockett). Pastor, if you are helping your church be a gospel lighthouse in a dark and sinful world, what you are doing is right. Go ahead, and don't let resistance stop you.

Here's a look forward to the remaining
"ESSENTIALS of a *Truly* Evangelistic Church":

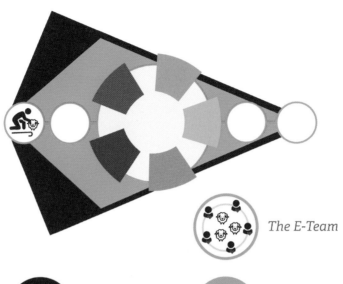

 The E-Team

 THE Mission   Local Focus

 Congregational   Equipped
Warmth   Congregation

 Basic   Peer
Discipleship   Accountability

 Evangelistic   Shared
Praying   Rejoicing

 Strategic   Relentless
Simplicity   Pursuit

Essential 1
Reflect & Act

Reflect:

1. Reread II Timothy 4:5. Why did Paul feel compelled to exhort Timothy to "do the work of an evangelist"?

2. What are some reasons the senior/lead pastor might be tempted to delegate evangelism initiatives of the church to other people?

3. What keeps someone from consistently going after lost sheep?

4. What are some benefits of the senior/lead pastor leading the way in the church's evangelism efforts?

Act:

1. Make a list of those with whom you are attempting to develop a redemptive relationship. Honestly, how much time each week do you devote to these?

2. What could you do that would encourage you and other church members to be more consistent in sharing their faith with unbelievers?

3. What step do you need to take next in response to this chapter?

4. What challenges might you encounter in implementing this essential in your church? How might you counter them?

Essential 2
The E-Team

*Building a Core Group of Christians
with Good-Shepherd Hearts*

***Buy-in and participation from a core group of members from the
congregation is important. No, it's ESSENTIAL! This is the pastor's first
and possibly most challenging task—identify and recruit an E-Team from
the congregation, folks who have a heart for lost sheep.***

Peer leadership (or should I call it pew leadership?) adds credibility to
pastoral leadership in essential Christian tasks such as personal evangelism.

It is easy for people in the pew to think evangelism is solely the pastor's
job. While some church members may enjoy hearing the pastor share his
personal experiences in building redemptive relationships and pointing
people to Jesus, they may assume it is his theological training and Bible
knowledge that makes it possible for him to evangelize effectively—
"Because he's a professional."

What they don't realize is that, in some ways, the non-theologically trained
folks in the congregation have more potential than their pastor to be
fruitful personal witnesses for Jesus.

A lot of unbelievers keep pastors at an arm's length because of what the
word *pastor* connotes to them. While, on the other hand, most regular
church members already have relationships with unbelievers—neighbors,
coworkers, friends, and relatives—who know and trust them.

If one or more ordinary members of the congregation begins to imitate the pastor's evangelistic lifestyle, the fever for seeing people's lives changed by the gospel will become increasingly contagious. With a little help from the pew, the "evangelism is (only) the pastor's job" myth can be demythologized.

I'm not going to say this will always be easy, but I think the process is fairly simple. At the risk of making this sound simplistic, let me suggest four steps.

Step One **Pray and identify potential members of a good shepherd core group, the beginnings of an E-Team.**

Throughout my more than 50 years of ministry, I have found at least a few people in every church I've been a part of—from a small country church, to a large multisite church—who have hearts for lost sheep. These are the people who:

- Often ask prayer for lost friends or loved ones.

- Share occasional stories of unbelievers to whom they are witnessing.

- Live consistent and boldly-Christian lives amidst a lot of unbelievers, on the job or elsewhere.

- Invite unsaved friends or family members to church, perhaps for special events, such as Christmas and Easter services.

- Respond positively when you mention the possibility of providing evangelism training.

These are the kinds of people to be looking for initially. I suggest that you personally chat with these folks and gauge their interest in meeting with you to pray and to discuss how *we* can help *our* church be more broadly active in reaching *our* communities with God's wonderful message of hope.

Step Two **Engage the initial evangelistic core group in praying the Harvester's Prayer.**

A Good-Shepherd pastor may only be able to reach one lost sheep at a time. And even a core group of church members whose hearts are in tune with the Shepherd's heart will need to expand. In fact, the most reliable indicator that a congregation is making progress toward becoming a *truly* evangelistic church is the gradual expansion of this core group. Expand the core with genuinely committed Christians; that's a key mark of progress!

Jesus left us with a how-to for expanding an evangelistic core group. It's the way He built his E-Team. I call it the "Harvester's Prayer."

> 36 When **he saw** the crowds, **he had compassion** for them, because they were **harassed** and **helpless**, like **sheep without a shepherd**.
> 37 *Then he said to his disciples, "The harvest is **plentiful**, but the laborers are few;*
> 38 *therefore **pray earnestly** to the Lord of the harvest to **send out** laborers into his harvest."*
>
> Matthew 9:36-38

Praying the Harvester's Prayer, works on two levels. Obviously, it is a plea to the Lord of the harvest to "send out laborers." "Send out" (ἐκβάλλω in Greek) is stronger than it sounds in English. It literally means to "drive out," "push out," or "thrust out with great impulse or force,"—even used with reference to "casting out" demons. It suggests overcoming strong resistance.

I don't know about you, but my selfish, introverted, want-to-be-liked self resists evangelism. God can and God does work on the hearts of Christians, through earnest prayer, to push through that resistance. That's the first reason we pray the Harvester's Prayer.

Also, prayers directed to the Lord of the harvest work in the hearts of pray-ers, the people who are praying this prayer. It helps embolden them (us!) to push through their (our!) own resisting impulses when God opens doors that might lead to redemptive conversations and conversion discussions.

But who were these harassed, helpless, and directionless people—a huge crowd of them? They were common folks who were harassed by the Roman government and led astray by spiritually blind religious leaders. They were helpless pawns in the powerful hands of Rome and institutional Judaism. They were beaten down by secular forces, confused by religious laws and rituals—so much so, they were just generally hopeless. They followed

Jesus because He offered a hopeful alternative, the same hope we have to offer the crowds of our generation who live with different, but basically similar, needs.

In our day, it is very easy to see the "crowd" and not see their needs. Their comfortable houses, nice automobiles, and fashionable attire are deceptive—these externals mask their spiritual needs. But if they are not genuine *born again* Christians, they are sheep without the Shepherd, lost and clinging to an eternally dangerous precipice.

As it did with Jesus, seeing beyond their exteriors to their deep spiritual needs is what produces compassion in our hearts. I suspect you have heard more emphasis on "the laborers are few" than "the harvest is plentiful." And that is unfortunate, because it overlooks the positive side of the challenge we face.

> *God, our Lord of the Harvest, please help us—all of us who want to rescue the lost sheep in our lives from the precipice of eternal damnation—to see beyond their external goodness, generosity, and cultural sophistication, to see them as YOU see them—spiritually harassed, helpless, and directionless without THE Shepherd.*

Jesus was probably thinking of wheat fields, but I'll change the agricultural metaphor a bit to be more visually understandable for most of us. Think of a huge apple orchard loaded down with ready-to-pick apples. **The ripe apples are there!** But if there are only two or three "pickers," the harvest will be disappointing. Multiply the pickers and the fruit of the harvest will become increasingly plentiful.

We can't blame the lack of conversions in our churches on the Biblical illiteracy and pluralism in our postmodern, post-Christian culture. The "harvest is plentiful," today as it was in the first century Roman world. Yes, there is some low hanging fruit, but much of it requires a lot more effort and patience to be picked.

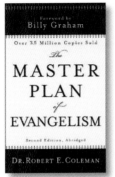

One of the all-time classic books on this topic is Robert Coleman's *The Master Plan of Evangelism.* Coleman expounded on the method Jesus used to achieve what our churches need to do. It's a simple method really: find a few committed followers of Jesus and train them to reach and train others, who will reach and train others (ad infinitum). The concept is so Biblically apparent and simple, why haven't more pastors implemented this "Master Plan" of Jesus in their churches?

Once a committed core group begins to gel, the next step is training. Jesus trained His core E-Team before training the broader group of His followers. And we can't go wrong by emulating His methodology. More will be said about a broader congregational training in a later chapter, but it's best to begin with the emerging E-Team.

Initial Training. Start with the Evangelism Essentials Visual Model. Present the model to the group and explain each facet, step-by-step, building the model as you go. As you lead the group through each ESSENTIAL, talk about implementation tactics for your church:

- What are the challenges we may face?

- What are some possible ways to counter these challenges?

- What are some additional ideas related to each ESSENTIAL that are not mentioned in the article?

- What are the practical steps to follow in getting started?

Prepare yourself for some "it won't work here" resistance, but don't let that discourage or defeat you. At this point you don't want to get mired down on any singular point. Just introduce the concepts with enough detail for them to gain a general understanding. Give them the overview, the BIG picture. To help with a later more-in-depth training series based on the Evangelism Essentials Model, we have prepared a Leader's Guide for you: www.GoodSoil.com/TEC-LG.pdf

Every local church is different, with different challenges in the process of evangelistic mobilization. Encourage your E-Team to be a part of tackling these challenges with you.

Next Step Training. One proven-to-be-effective way to equip your "twelve" (or however many are in your E-Team) is to accompany them to a Good Soil Evangelism and Discipleship Seminar. Not only will they be personally trained to share God's story of hope in a world of competing faiths and cultures, but, on the third day of the seminar week, they will be trained and certified to team-teach the Basic Good Soil Seminar with you back in your church.

As a gesture of our desire to help you implement the "Master's plan of evangelism" in your church, we extend this special offer to you:

> *If you are a pastor and can bring at least two other church members from your congregation with you, we invite* **YOU** *and the* **OTHER MEMBERS** *(regardless of how many that might be) to attend FREE, if you attend all three days together. Register yourself using the promotional code* **"Pastor"** *and have the others register separately using this same code. (This offer may not be extended forever.)*

Step Four **Engage the E-Team in leadership roles, based on their gifts and skills.**

Engage members of the E-Team in helping you lead the church through this process of becoming a more-*truly* evangelistic church. But be sure that the person has demonstrated ability to perform an assigned task.

As you read the remaining articles in this series, be thinking about how you can share the load of these responsibilities with your team. The more they are engaged, the stronger their commitment will be.

Here's a look forward to the remaining
"ESSENTIALS of a *Truly* Evangelistic Church":

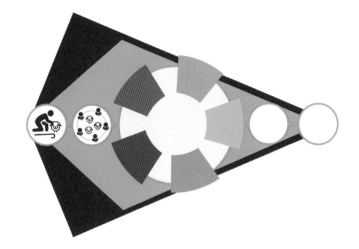

 THE Mission

 Local Focus

 Congregational Warmth

 Equipped Congregation

 Basic Discipleship

 Peer Accountability

 Evangelistic Praying

 Shared Rejoicing

 Strategic Simplicity

 Relentless Pursuit

Essential 2
Reflect & Act

Reflect:

1. Why is "peer leadership," as defined in this chapter, essential for success in local church evangelism?

2. What benefits do you see in initially pursuing the core members for your E-Team, rather than just asking for volunteers?

3. Which of the steps in this chapter do you find most challenging? Why?

Act:

1. Make a list of the qualities and characteristics you would look for in building an E-Team.

2. Prayerfully identify 2 – 6 individuals that you might ask to be a part of the E-Team.

3. Lay out what you see as a reasonable time frame to accomplish the four steps in this chapter.

4. What step do you need to take next in response to this chapter?

5. What challenges might you encounter in implementing this essential in your church? How might you counter them?

Essential 3

THE Mission

Making the Great Commission THE Mission of Your Church

A local church's mission must truly be the Great Commission. Just using the "Great Commission" as a pious platitude is not enough.

If a church ministry researcher, an objective outsider, visited every service and activity of your church for one month, what would he or she report is the *true* mission of your church?

In the business world, secret shoppers (also called mystery shoppers) are hired to give objective professional feedback on how a store is *really* doing. What kind of review would your church get if a *Great Commission* secret shopper "shopped" at your church?

Virtually every evangelical church states somewhere in an official church document that it exists to carry out the Great Commission. But a 2018 Barna survey found that 51% of U.S. churchgoers said they were not familiar with the term "Great Commission." Another 25% indicated they had heard the term but could not recall its exact meaning. And only 37% could pick Matthew 28:18-20 out of a "line up" among four other unrelated Bible passages as being a Great Commission text.

Do you really and truly want to know whether or not your church is a Great Commission church? If that is important to you, ask yourself the following five questions and be brutally honest with your answers. And, if you are a pastor, guide your church leaders in a frank discussion based on these questions:

> [18] And Jesus came and said to them, "All authority in heaven and on earth has been given to me. [19] Go therefore and make disciples of all nations, baptizing them in the name of the Father and of the Son and of the Holy Spirit, [20] teaching them to observe all that I have commanded you. And behold, I am with you always, to the end of the age."
>
> Matthew 28:18-20

First—Is your church actively "going" in the way Jesus intended in His commission?

[1]Go—

As simple as the Great Commission appears to be, a lot of Christians have spent far too much time and ink trying to understand and explain it—often with the result of confusing and misinterpreting its simple meaning. Years ago, someone told me, "The way to understand the meaning of the Great Commission is to read the Book of Acts and see how the early church understood it." Try that if you have doubts about the meaning and seriousness of our Lord's commission. For example:

> [1] And there arose on that day a great persecution against the church in Jerusalem, and they were all scattered throughout the regions of Judea and Samaria, except the apostles.
>
> [4] Now those who were scattered went about preaching the word.
>
> Acts 8: 1,4

But what should "Go" mean today, in your church and mine? How are we to contextualize obedience to the Great Commission in our congregations at the local level? We will continue to explore this idea, but the following are a few thoughts to get us started. If your church is "Going," in the Great Commission sense...

- A high percentage of your church members will be practicing evangelism as a regular lifestyle. And I don't mean just being nonverbal witnesses. They will be talking to unbelievers about Jesus and how He can give them eternal hope and bring joy into their lives.
- Seeker-unbelievers and newly reborn folks will be showing up in your church services frequently, instead of rarely.
- Your church will be thinking *outwardly* as much, or more than, *inwardly*. Church members will be looking for opportunities to bring their unsaved friends to church and any of its seeker-friendly activities.

Second—Is your church making disciples?

¹Go—²*make disciples*

In much of western Christianity today, the word *discipleship* has become very popular, much more popular than the word *evangelism.* That's probably because *evangelism* and *conversion* and *saved* and *born-again* are not politically correct in our pluralistic societies, but *discipleship* has not yet been blacklisted by liberal politicians, media, and religious leaders. And discipleship with other Christians is not as intimidating as telling an unbeliever his or her worldview is wrong and there are serious eternal consequences for not putting complete trust in Jesus Christ--the *one and only Way* to receive eternal life.

Discipleship, in many evangelical churches today, means one of two things: (1) doing one-on-one spiritual mentoring with an immature believer, or (2) small group Christian Bible studies focused on issues related to spiritual growth.

Please do not misunderstand me—those ARE good and important ministries. But that is not the core command of the Great Commission.

To understand the meaning of "make disciples," look at the two participles that follow the command to disciplize. The first is "baptizing." What precedes baptizing? Conversion!

Another way to understand the meaning of "make disciples" in Matthew's account of the Great Commission is to compare it with the accounts given by Mark and Luke:

> ¹⁵ **And he said to them, "Go into all the world and proclaim the gospel to the whole creation.**
> Mark 16:15

> ⁴⁵ Then he opened their minds to understand the Scriptures, ⁴⁶ and said to them, "Thus it is written, that the Christ should suffer and on the third day rise from the dead, ⁴⁷ and that **repentance for the forgiveness of sins should be proclaimed in his name** to all nations, beginning from Jerusalem. ⁴⁸ **You are witnesses of these things."**
> Luke 24:45-48

> ⁸ "But you will receive power when the Holy Spirit has come upon you, and **you will be my witnesses** in Jerusalem and in all Judea and Samaria, and to the end of the earth."
> Acts 1:8

When Jesus commanded us to make disciples, He meant for us to do our human part in making followers of Jesus—followers who followed because they believed in Him, had turned from their previous religious beliefs and practices, and simultaneously put their trust in Him. In other words, He meant for us to begin by evangelizing.

To focus on discipleship (in the all-too-often modern sense), without prioritizing evangelism, is not a Biblically balanced response to the Great Commission.

After all, where are your potential "disciples" if your church is not actively engaged in bringing sinners to faith in Jesus?

¹Go—²make disciples
—³of various people groups

When we read Matthew 28:18-20, our tendency is to think of *nations* as *countries*. But the New Testament word for *nations (ethne)* means *people groups*, not political entities with geographical boundaries.

Yes, there is the "to the end of the earth" scope of the Great Commission, as Jesus indicated in Acts 1:8. That's foreign missions, a vital part of the command that every *truly* evangelistic church will be involved in obeying.

 But, even in North America, there are "nations" all around most of our churches—people groups with skin colors, languages, customs, and social connections that are very different from most of the members of our congregations. The topic is too big to get into in this article, but John Piper's *Let the Nations Be Glad* informs us that "all the nations" outreach *can* and *should* be local, as well as global.

Is your church reaching and assimilating members of local people groups who do not typically identify with the ethnic demography of your congregation's core membership?

Fourth—Do the professions of faith that happen through your church's ministry result in baptisms?

¹Go—²make disciples
—³of various people groups
—and ⁴baptize them

I know of churches that practice a style of evangelism that results in lots of *decisions*, but few baptisms. Something is seriously wrong if people who profess faith in Jesus are not willing to identify with Christ and His Church by baptism. And there is something wrong with churches if their approaches to evangelism are resulting in many profess-ers, but few disciples.

One key indicator of a *truly* evangelistic church is a regular occurrence of new believers who are identifying publicly, through baptism, as sincere followers of Jesus Christ. Yes, it is a wonderful thing to watch the children of your church's families profess their faith in Jesus and follow Him in baptism. But if those are the only baptisms happening in your church, it is probably a sign that your church is inwardly focused, not *truly* evangelistic in the Great Commission sense.

Fifth—Is your church a Great Commission "Teaching" Church?

¹Go—²make disciples —³of various people groups —and ⁴baptize them
—and ⁵teach them.

Here's where what many Christians now think of as *discipleship* comes in. Just as a church cannot claim to be a Great Commission church without *evangelism* (which results in baptisms), it also can't claim to be a Great Commission church without solid *teaching* (teaching that matures its disciples to be healthy disciples-who-make-other-disciples).

To be accurate in interpreting Matthew 28:18-20, we need to ask, "Teaching whom?" In this context, Jesus was specifically telling us to teach those whom we have reached, who have been converted (from among a variety of available people groups), to be genuine faith-based Christ-followers (who have been baptized).

For many churches, teaching is simply stuffing more Bible knowledge into heads of pew-sitters who already know a lot but do little to practice what they know. Great Commission teaching, as Jesus intended, is more about grounding new believers in the Word of God, so they can effectively obey the same commission that brought them to Jesus, as His disciples.

With all of this in mind, what would a "secret shopper" say about your church?

Here's a look forward to the remaining
"ESSENTIALS of a *Truly* Evangelistic Church":

Local Focus

Congregational Warmth

Equipped Congregation

Basic Discipleship

Peer Accountability

Evangelistic Praying

Shared Rejoicing

Strategic Simplicity

Relentless Pursuit

Essential 3

Reflect & Act

Reflect:

1. Considering the Barna Group survey, how well do churches understand that the Great Commission must be the primary mission?

2. How often do we hear about those in our churches actively reaching out to lost sheep?

3. Do you agree that prioritizing evangelism is important for making disciples?

4. What indicators would determine whether a local church has the Great Commission as its REAL mission?

Act:

1. Does your church's mission statement make plain the importance of the Great Commission?

2. Determine the best way to find out what percentage of your church's congregation is practicing evangelism as a regular part of their daily life.

3. Evaluate the Bible teaching believers receive at your church. How much is helping them to effectively carry out the Great Commission?

4. What step do you need to take next in response to this chapter?

5. What challenges might you encounter in implementing this essential in your church? How might you counter them?

Essential 4
Local Focus

Lead Your Church to Bloom
Where It Was Planted

A local church must not jump over the "Jerusalem" of Acts 1:8 to try to salve its congregational conscience by only supporting foreign missions. A church's first and foremost responsibility is to "bloom where it was planted."

Did you ever stop and think, *"Why was my church planted where it was planted?"* If you were to trace the history of your church back to its beginning, what would you find that motivated the men and women who took a step of faith to begin your church?

In many cases, you would probably discover that someone or some group of people realized the community where your church was planted *needed* a church—a lighthouse beaming the saving gospel of Jesus throughout the surrounding neighborhoods. Chances are, the need is still there—perhaps more than ever before.

Local Churches with Presbyopia

Presbyopia–It may not be a term that you are familiar with, but it's a reality that all of us will eventually have to deal with if we haven't already. Presbyopia is the normal loss of near-focusing ability that occurs with age.

Our loss of near-focusing happens so gradually that we don't know it's gone until the results become so intolerable that we can't go on without getting help. I never needed glasses until my early adult years when I began to realize I was becoming only near-focused. I could read without glasses but couldn't read the road signs. With the help from my optometrist and optician, the far-focus in my vision gradually improved. Now I can read road signs without glasses but, because of my aging eyes, I can't read the book I'm holding in my hands or the computer screen right in front of me without something to help me with *presbyopia*.

Many evangelical churches that I'm familiar with have had a similar experience. They were planted because the founders clearly saw the need around them, but now their local focus has dimmed. Because they do have some commitment to the Great Commission, they have shifted their vision and focus to giving support for evangelism, discipleship, and church planting "over there."

I know of national church leaders from outside North America who have visited some of their North American supporting churches. These churches sent missionaries to other nations to teach them to evangelize, disciple, and plant churches. Often these church leaders from other countries are shocked and disappointed that the churches who sent missionaries to them are not practicing themselves what they have sent those very missionaries to do.

Please don't misunderstand me. I am very committed to international missions. For 25 years I have worked for an international mission agency. I've had the privilege of teaching and training missionaries and national leaders in over 30 countries. My personal ministry would not have been possible without the faithful and sometimes sacrificial support of Christian families and local churches in North America. But a local church's commitment to foreign missions should not become a cop-out for ignoring doing missions in the community where the church was planted.

Yes, Jesus said, "all the world," and, "the whole creation," in Mark 16:15. He said, "all nations," in Matthew 28:19 and Luke 24:47. He said, "to the end of the earth," in Acts 1:8. But, to clarify the expectations of this commission, He said:

> **"...beginning from Jerusalem."**
> Luke 24:47

> **"...you will be my witnesses in Jerusalem..."**
> Acts 1:8

In Chapter Two, I shared some thoughts about the Harvester's Prayer in Matthew 9. The same prayer-exhortation also occurs in Luke 10 from another event in the ministry of Jesus.

> **Commissioning of the Twelve, in Galilee:**
> 36 When he saw the crowds, he had compassion for them, because they were harassed and helpless, like sheep without a shepherd. 37 Then he said to his disciples, *"The harvest is plentiful, but the laborers are few; 38 therefore pray earnestly to the Lord of the harvest to send out laborers into his harvest."*
> Matthew 9:36-38

> **Sending Out the Seventy-Two in Judea:**
> 1After this the Lord appointed seventy-two others and sent them on ahead of him, two by two, into every town and place where he himself was about to go. 2And he said to them, *"The harvest is plentiful, but the laborers are few. Therefore pray earnestly to the Lord of the harvest to send out laborers into his harvest."*
> Luke 10:1-2

Notice carefully: These were two different events in two different locations at two different times and recorded by two different apostles, but the need for harvesters and exhortations by Jesus were *exactly* the same—word for word in many English translations because the exact same Greek words were recorded by Matthew and Luke.

I've heard dozens of sermons on these passages, but—if I recall correctly—most, if not all, of them have been missionary sermons, challenging Christians to consider becoming missionaries to foreign fields. There's nothing wrong with using these texts in that way, but **here the focus was local** for Jesus. He saw the crowds in **Galilee**, which moved Him to pray for harvesters. He sent disciples into towns and villages of **Judea**, realizing the need for more harvesters.

On another occasion, this time in **Samaria**, Jesus pointed His disciples to the ripe harvest fields all around them. In this instance, Jesus was telling His followers to "lift up their eyes" to see those coming toward them from town whom the woman invited to come meet Jesus. Think *local focus!*

> **Seekers in Samaria:**
> [35] "Do you not say, 'There are yet four months, then comes the harvest?' Look, I tell you, lift up your eyes, and see that the fields are white for harvest."
> John 4:35

Your Church's Here:There Ratio

The term *glocal* has become popular in recent years among economists, politicians, and even missiologists and church leaders. It means to simultaneously give appropriate attention to the *here* and the *there*—the local and the foreign. Think McDonalds, KFC, Coca Cola, Pizza Hut, Exxon & Shell & BP, not to mention tech companies like Apple, Microsoft, Google, etc.

How successful would McDonalds and Coca Cola be, if they didn't balance the *here* and the *there*?

Jesus didn't invent the term *glocal*, but he certainly endorsed the concept and commanded its implementation for the spread of the gospel.

There is no perfect survey instrument to determine how balanced your church's *Here:There* ratio is. But it shouldn't take you and your church's leadership long to assess it well enough to know whether or not you are "blooming where you were planted."

- What percentage of your church's programs are genuinely (*genuinely*) focused on spreading the gospel to your local community?
- It's not all about money and the budget, but how much of your church's budget is allocated to local evangelistic outreach?
- What percentage, roughly speaking, of your church members are actively developing relationships locally with unbelievers with a goal of presenting the gospel to them when they are open to receiving it?
- How many lives of folks from your church's local neighborhood are you seeing changed through the ministry of your church?

I hear you thinking, *"But you don't know how difficult it is to evangelize in our area! You don't understand that people where we are don't want to hear about God, the Bible, or Jesus!" Or: "Everybody around our church has their own religion!"*

If we really thought those excuses were valid, we wouldn't send missionaries to most parts of the world. But because the "gospel…is the power of God for salvation to everyone who believes," there is no place too hard for the gospel to work when combined with planting, prayer, and patience—*even where you live!*

Renewing and Improving Your Church's Local Focus

Are you concerned that your church seems to have lost its local focus? Are you concerned enough to take steps to regain or strengthen it? Many pastors and congregational members are concerned, even to the point of near-desperation. We, at Good Soil Evangelism and Discipleship, often hear those pleas for help.

There is hope. Your church can regain its life-changing impact on the community in which your church was planted—it CAN bloom there again. That's the reason for this book.

If the pastor is willing to lead the effort and he has rallied a core group of evangelistically interested members of the congregation who want to make the Great Commission the TRUE mission of the church (locally as well as internationally), there is definite hope, realistic hope.

The next step is to develop a strategy for reaching your "Jerusalem" the way Jesus intended and the way the early church responded. But a strategy must be customized—it must be localized for your church and your community. In these chapters, we can only give you the tested and proven principles upon which you can build your own local strategy.

The first four chapters covered foundational principles:
- **The Pastor** must lead the church in its effort to become a *truly* evangelistic church.
- **E-Team** support (peer leadership) is essential to spreading the passion and exemplifying the possibilities throughout the congregation.
- **THE Mission** of the church must REALLY be the Great Commission, not just a pious platitude hidden away in the church's constitution.
- **Local Focus** must not be neglected, even if the church has the far-sight to support missionaries "over there."

The next eight chapters will give you the practical how-to principles for customizing a localized evangelistic strategy so that your church can, and will, "bloom where it was planted."

Here's a look forward to the remaining
"ESSENTIALS of a *Truly* Evangelistic Church":

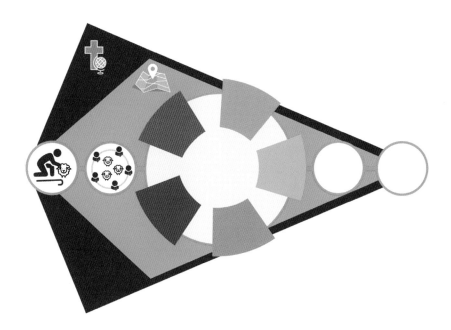

 Congregational
Warmth

 Equipped
Congregation

 Basic
Discipleship

 Peer
Accountability

 Evangelistic
Praying

 Shared
Rejoicing

 Strategic
Simplicity

 Relentless
Pursuit

Essential 4
Reflect & Act

Reflect:

1. Do you know the history of the beginning of your church and what motivated those who started it?

2. What is *presbyopia*? Why would it be a problem for a local church?

3. What excuses are given for a church not "blooming where it was planted?"

4. How would you explain the importance of being *glocal*?

Act:

1. Do a quick assessment of your church's *Here:There* ratio.

2. List the programs of your church which have, as their primary focus, taking the gospel to your local community.

3. Conduct a study of the people groups in your church's area. Which of these do you think your church is better prepared to reach?

4. What step do you need to take next in response to this chapter?

5. What challenges might you encounter in implementing this essential in your church? How might you counter them?

Congregational Warmth

Developing a Culture of
Authentic Hospitality

A church that doesn't warmly embrace its visitors can't be truly evangelistic.

"Alien tissue rejection"— I first learned about the tendency for the human body to reject a transplanted organ when one of my best friends had a heart transplant several years ago. The body recognizes the transplanted tissue as foreign and persistently mounts an immune response to reject it.

Many congregations respond in a similar way to visitors, to varying degrees. But a church that doesn't warmly embrace its visitors – can't be *truly* evangelistic. In this chapter you will learn about Five Congregational Temperatures and how to set your church's "thermostat" at the best setting to make new attenders feel at home and want to come back.

You have probably experienced some, if not all, of these Five Congregational Temperatures. As I was working on this graph, specific churches that I have visited over the years spontaneously came to my mind. Try to think of your church, from a visitor's perspective.

This will not be easy for many churches. Think of the office or home where there is someone who is more comfortable with the thermostat setting at 66 than 72. Then there are others who complain with any setting under 78.

In a similar way, church congregations consist of members with differing preferences for visitor-warmth. Some of them, by personality or by

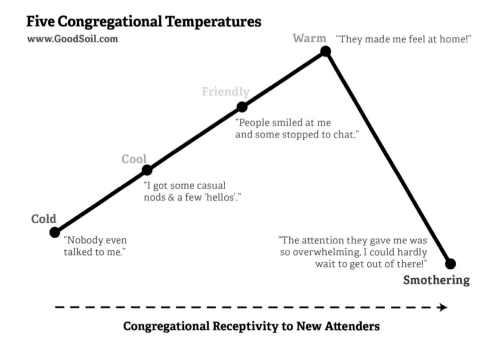

Five Congregational Temperatures

www.GoodSoil.com

Warm   "They made me feel at home!"

Friendly

"People smiled at me
and some stopped to chat."

Cool

"I got some casual
nods & a few 'hellos'."

Cold

"Nobody even
talked to me."

"The attention they gave me was
so overwhelming, I could hardly
wait to get out of there!"

Smothering

Congregational Receptivity to New Attenders

personal conviction, really want to make visitors feel right at home. Other members are perfectly fine with a congregational climate that freezes out visitors. Adjustments to visitor-warmth will require teaching, training, and time. But the results will be worth the effort.

Prepare. First, take a look at your church's facilities, inside and out, and think how welcome you would feel if you were a visitor, perhaps an unchurched person, visiting your church for the first time. Are there convenient parking spaces reserved for visitors? Is the entrance clearly marked and easy to find?

Then, when you enter the building, would you know where to go? Nursery? Restrooms? Worship Center? Where would you find layout or mission statement information about this church?

Second, think about the congregational welcome—how warmly would the members of your church receive you if you were a complete stranger, maybe from an ethnic minority not commonly represented in your congregation? Or what if your appearance was not traditionally church-like?

There are some churches for which congregational warmth is not a problem, because of the personalities of the members and spiritual sensitivity to the needs of people who visit. But many church members need to be taught and trained to practice what the New Testament teaches about Christian hospitality—hospitality that places the visitor's feelings and needs above ours.

> [7] *Therefore welcome one another as Christ has welcomed you, for the glory of God.*
> Romans 15:7
>
> [35] *...I was a stranger and you welcomed me.*
> Matthew 25:35
>
> [13] *Contribute to the needs of the saints and seek to show hospitality.*
> Romans 12:13
>
> [2] *Do not neglect to show hospitality to strangers...*
> Hebrews 13:2
>
> [4] *Let each of you look not only to his own interests, but also the interests of other.*
> Philippians 2:4

I can't say it any better than this:

> *"How do we treat our visitors? This is one of the first questions that must be asked by any congregation that is thinking seriously about evangelism. It hardly makes sense to develop strategies for inviting people to church if we don't know how to treat the people who come on their own."*
>
> *- Harold Percy*

Invite. As your congregational temperature nears or reaches the *warmth* level, church members will feel more at ease inviting friends. And it's a good idea to plan a few Red Carpet programs or activities each year that are easy-to-invite-to events—concerts, seasonal programs, fun nights, etc.

Setting your church's thermostat is not only about making visitors feel at home, it is also crucial in helping new believers assimilate into the congregational fellowship of your church. It's a key step in what we think of as basic discipleship.

Embrace. By *embrace*, I don't mean hugging. That would freak me and many others out! But everyone needs to *feel embraced*, in whatever way is most comfortable and safe for him or her. Here's where your church members will need to be taught and trained.

Teach them how to read a new attender's comfort with personal attention and how to respond accordingly.

- Some shy visitors will be most happy with very little attention. Be friendly and warm but give them space.

- Some visitors will expect and desire to be engaged in friendly conversation, but will not want to go too deep, too quickly. Avoid pressing the conversation; let them lead it.

- Other, more gregarious, visitors may freely initiate conversations with no reservations. Use those opportunities to learn about them, rather than tell them all about you.

- Occasionally, there will be visitors who are desperate for help and a shoulder to cry on. Express your interest and concern but avoid getting involved too deeply or making commitments before you learn more about them.

One pastor defined the difference between a friendly church and a warm church in one word: *relationships*. But then he broke the distinctions down more specifically:

> *There is a difference between a friendly church and a warm church. A friendly church greets everyone, a warm church accepts anyone. A friendly church calls everyone by name; a warm church takes the time to learn about everyone named. A friendly church is ready with church information; a warm church is ready to discover information about the person.*
>
> - Mark Erskine

Welcome Back. In previous generations, a follow-up visit by the pastor to the visitor's home was in vogue and maybe even expected—now, not so much. In some settings, a phone call to follow up might be appropriate, but not in all cases. A personalized handwritten note would rarely be unwelcome.

But the best "welcome back" is not written or spoken. The most genuine re-invitation occurs when the visitor leaves the church *feeling welcome* to come again, but not pressured to do so.

Assimilate. The polar opposite of rejection is assimilation. In local church terms, assimilation means to be accepted into the body as a fully-belonging person. In a small congregation, a new member may realize a sense of assimilation into the whole congregation in a relatively short period of time. In larger congregations, assimilation occurs more quickly in a small group of some sort—Bible class, home fellowship group, choir, church sports team, special events cooking group, nursery team, etc.

The feeling of being an insider with a network of friends is the essence of assimilation. It is important to provide assimilation opportunities for anyone who shows an interest in belonging within your congregation.

Starter List of Suggestions

There is no specific predefined plan that will work for every church, but there is also no dearth of ideas available to you. Google "friendly church," or "warm church," or "church hospitality" and you will discover that many church leaders have wrestled with this issue and have discovered and created more good ideas that you will ever be able to use. Here's a list of some of them:

1. Preach a series of sermons on Christian hospitality as taught in the New Testament and practiced in the New Testament Church. Laying a Biblical foundation is a good first step.
2. Model congregational warmth as a pastor and pastoral staff. Mix and mingle with the congregation, especially new attenders, before and after each service. Don't teach and preach it if you won't practice it.
3. Start with a select group of trained greeters, people for whom greeting comes naturally, but make "every member a greeter" your goal.

4. Create a hospitality committee and, with their help, develop a plan to set and maintain the proper level of congregational warmth.

5. Do a thorough and systematic visitor readiness assessment of your facilities, inside and out.

6. Properly positioned and staffed welcome centers can assist with church information, directions, and answers to visitors' questions; but a welcome center does not replace other vital hospitality features.

7. Lead some teaching (information) and training (practice) sessions, at times when the core of your congregation is assembled. Repeat occasionally.

8. Teach members to think of the zone around where they normally sit and encourage them to take responsibility for Christian hospitality in their zones.

9. Constantly be aware of the level of congregational warmth and deal with cooling off when you sense it is happening. "Nip it in the bud."

10. Establish a feedback process for visitors, perhaps based on the five congregational temperatures. More than anyone, they know how warm or cool your church really is.

Here's a look forward to the remaining
"ESSENTIALS of a *Truly* Evangelistic Church":

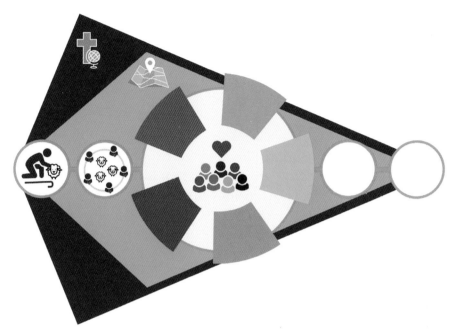

 Equipped
Congregation

 Basic
Discipleship

 Peer
Accountability

 Evangelistic
Praying

 Shared
Rejoicing

 Strategic
Simplicity

 Relentless
Pursuit

Essential 5

Reflect & Act

Reflect:

1. How do you react to this statement by Harold Percy? *"How do we treat our visitors? This is one of the first questions that must be asked by any congregation that is thinking seriously about evangelism. It hardly makes sense to develop strategies for inviting people to church if we don't know how to treat the people who come on their own."*

2. What is the difference between a friendly church and a warm church?

3. What Red Carpet events can you think of that your church has done?

4. What is necessary to assimilate new people into a church's body life?

Act:

1. What might need to change for your church to become a *warm* church?

2. Make a list of Red Carpet events that would draw people from your area.

3. What kind of *Welcome Back* contact do you think would work best with unbelievers who visit your church?

Essential 6
Equipped Congregation

Arming the Church with Appropriate
Training and Resources

Our military leaders know that training is the foundation for success in combat. They would never send their personnel into battle without proper training and the best available resources.

How well do we equip our church members for spiritual warfare—particularly the battle to rescue lost souls?

Many of you who read this are shepherds (pastors) or teachers. I assume that virtually all of you are saints (true born-again believers) who have been commissioned by our Lord to do the work of ministering. In one of the most important directives for church ministry in all of the New Testament, the Apostle Paul clearly stated the responsibility of church leaders to prepare believers for ministry.

> [11] And he gave the apostles, the prophets, the evangelists, the shepherds and teachers, [12] **to equip the saints for the work of ministry...**
> Ephesians 4:11-12

The original Greek word for *equip* that Paul used is only found in this one text in the New Testament. It means to *render effective* and *workable* something that is not yet in a condition to function as it should.

I remember the early months of my life as a Christian. It didn't take me long to realize I needed to (and wanted to) lead my unsaved friends to Jesus, but

I was not yet equipped. I didn't feel confident enough to explain how they could experience forgiveness of sin and receive eternal life, as I had. So I would share my story with them and then take them to my pastor's house— sometimes in the middle of the night—in order that he could explain the gospel to them and help them place their faith in Jesus. Thankfully, my pastor began to equip me for the ministry of evangelism. *He probably got tired of me knocking on his door and getting him out of bed near midnight or after!*

My guess is—there are Christians in your church who feel just as inadequate as I did, even though they were saved years ago. As a pastor-teacher, it is one of your most important jobs to *equip* your congregation for ministry, especially the Great Commission ministry. We would love to help you with that responsibility. And if you are a Christian who is not confident in explaining the gospel and helping unbelievers come to faith in Jesus, this article can help you too.

Five Keys for Effective Great Commission Equipping

First: As culture changes, the content and methods for Great Commission equipping must also change.

> *"Warfare is always changing, always evolving.*
> *Military training must, therefore, change as well."*
> - "Training: The Foundation for Success in Combat" (Heritage.org)
>
> Translated into church-talk:
> *"Evangelism training of yesteryear is not adequate for today."*

If you grew up in church prior to the last decade or two of the 20th Century, you would know that ministry was much different in those days than now. In earlier decades, most people in North America knew who God is, who Jesus is, what the Bible is all about. They were familiar with the stories of Adam and Eve, the true significance of Christmas, the Crucifixion and Easter story, etc.

Chances are there were not very many Muslims, Hindus, Buddhists, Spiritists, postmoderns, or hard-core atheists in your township, city, or county at that time. And most of the basic Biblical concepts, such as sin, salvation, heaven, and hell were generally known, albeit perhaps not clearly.

In those days, a presentation of the gospel of Jesus Christ could begin with:
"God loves you and has a wonderful plan for your life."

"If you stood before God and He asked you, 'Why should I let you into my heaven,' what would you say?"

"The Bible says, 'for all have sinned and come short of the glory of God.'"

The increasing degree of Biblical illiteracy in North America has necessitated a change in the way we explain the gospel to non-Christians. As followers of Jesus today, we all need to be equipped to share the Bible's big story, the historical-Biblical context for basic gospel truths. Otherwise, concepts such as *God, sin, Jesus died for you,* and *you need to be saved,* mean nothing to many contemporary North Americans. Evangelism training for today and the future must adapt to the increasingly secular and pluralistic cultural changes happening all around most of us.

"God's Eternal Plan," From The Way to Joy

The positive side of this otherwise depressing cultural change is that many Americans, including unbelievers, are curious about the Bible and want to know more. A recent American Bible Society survey revealed that 63% of Americans expressed some curiosity to know about the Bible and its teachings, with 29% registering a strong desire. Sixty-one percent were interested in knowing more about Jesus Christ.

Evangelism resources that promise Bible-curious non-Christians an opportunity to understand the overall message and meaning of the Bible can be an attractive way to engage them with God's redemptive story.

Second: **Evangelism training should blend 1. essential Bible-based content with 2. practical how-to techniques and 3. lifelike simulations, in preparation for 4. real-life opportunities to share the gospel.**

1. **Essential Bible-based Content:** Contrary to what some timid Christians may think, they don't need to be Bible scholars to lead unbelievers to Jesus, but some basic Biblical instruction is important. And if they use the appropriate evangelism resources, most of the Biblical content they need will be embedded in the resources.

2. **Practical How-To Techniques:** Some evangelism training programs consist of teaching trainees word-for-word sales pitches. And unbelievers recognize an advertisement from the first few words. Training for authentic evangelism is much more flexible. It provides basic tips for helping Christians be themselves in a way that doesn't force them into a methodological straitjacket. The best evangelism training and resources will balance method with individuality, structure with flexibility, and content with personalization—tips and techniques, not rote and rigid talking points.

3. **Lifelike Simulations:** In military training, "the goal is for military forces entering combat to have 'been there before' so that they can know how to win.'" Simulations are a safe way to help Christians feel like they have "been there before," before they encounter some of the common situations they fear are coming. In today's multicultural pluralistic societies, evangelism training should include simulations that prepare Christ-followers to share the gospel with people from a variety of non-Christian worldview settings. We call it worldview-relevant evangelism training.

4. **Real-life Evangelism Opportunities:** We can never prepare everyone for everything, but we can prepare evangelism trainees in how to react when they feel trapped, not knowing what to say. They need to practice saying, "I don't know, but I will find out." We should see their early "brick wall" experiences as teachable moments and provide the debriefing opportunities that will allow us to deepen and expand their training.

---

1   "Training: The Foundation for Success in Combat" from Heritage.org

Third: **Evangelism training should be transferable, clear and simple enough that once trained, a trainee can use it to train others– who can train others, who can train others.**

Transferability means to cause to pass from one person to another. It's the "I learn, now I train," learn-train, learn-train, learn-train process that Paul modeled and advocated.

> [2]...and what you have heard from me in the presence of many witnesses entrust to faithful men, who will be able to teach others also.
> 2 Timothy 2:2

Transferability has always been at the forefront of Good Soil philosophy and methodology. That is why we...

- Create free Leader's Guides and Class Facilitator Guides to accompany many of our evangelism and discipleship resources.
- Offer Good Soil Trainer Certification Workshops that follow our Basic Seminars.
- Developed **Gaining Ground with Good Soil**, which we think of as a *Good Soil Seminar in a story book*. Training resources to accompany that book are available as free downloads.

It is why we have embedded the essence of Good Soil training in visual models that make it easy for you to teach others what you have learned. We have made our three primary visual models available as free downloads from our website (www.GoodSoil.com/about/).

Fourth: **Evangelism training and resources should go hand in glove.**

Think of training as the *hands* and evangelism resources as the *gloves*. They both work better together when they are well-matched.

For example, military training is not

about rifles in general or generic parachutes. Military personnel are trained to use the rifle they will carry and the kind of parachute they will rely on when they make their jumps. Best practices training is matched to specific resources.

Good Soil's *The Story of Hope, The Way to Joy,* the *Chronological Bridge to Life, The Roots of Faith,* and all of its other evangelism and discipleship resources were custom-designed to be the *gloves* that fit the *hands* of Good Soil Basic Seminar training.

Fifth: You can't expect a one-time "boot camp" evangelism training to be all of the training your church members will ever need.

We have trained hundreds of pastors in Good Soil seminars—across North America and around the world. In virtually all cases, pastors leave Good Soil seminars excited about seeing their churches implement what they have learned. But, unfortunately, some of them never equip their congregations with the training and resources they learned in the seminar—they never take the first step of transferring. Thus, training for them is a dead-end street. Other pastors who do pass on some (or all) of the Good Soil training to their congregations assume a one-time experience is all they need to offer.

Ongoing training is vital—boosters, enhancers, refreshers, and extenders. And there are lots of ways (and resources) to keep our congregations "battle-ready." Good Soil Evangelism and Discipleship can help you with that.

> *"Soldiers, sailors, airmen, and Marines are trained from the first day they enter the armed forces until the last day of their service."*
>
> *"Training: The Foundation for Success in Combat" from Heritage.org*

May God help us as followers of Jesus to take our marching orders as seriously as the military. Eternal destinies are even more important than mortal lives!

Here's a look forward to the remaining
"ESSENTIALS of a *Truly* Evangelistic Church":

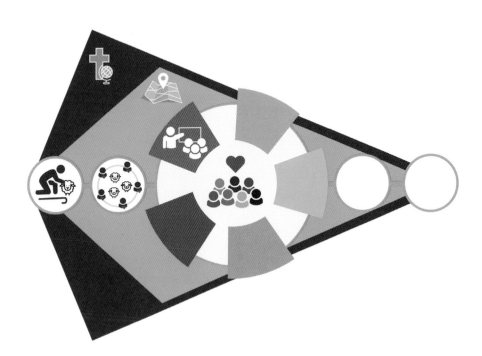

 Basic
Discipleship

 Peer
Accountability

 Evangelistic
Praying

 Shared
Rejoicing

 Strategic
Simplicity

 Relentless
Pursuit

Essential 6

Reflect & Act

Reflect:

1. According to Ephesians 4:11-12, the shepherd-teachers are "to equip the saints for the work of ministry." What does "equip" mean?

2. How capable do you feel at equipping your church in evangelism that meets the keys listed in this chapter? Would you want help?

3. Why are "word-for-word evangelistic sales pitches" not effective with most unbelievers today?

4. How important for a church is ongoing training in evangelism?

Act:

1. Which one of the keys to effective Great Commission equipping do you think will be the most challenging?

2. What training has your church provided for Great Commission equipping? When was it last provided? How effective has it been?

3. Visit the Good Soil "About" page (www.GoodSoil.com/About) to acquaint yourself with the Good Soil Evangelism and Discipleship theology, methodology, training, and resources.

4. What step do you need to take next in response to this chapter?

5. What challenges might you encounter in implementing this essential in your church? How might you counter them?

Essential 7

Basic Discipleship

Holding New Believers' Hands
Through Their First Steps

If your church doesn't provide "first steps" hand-holding with baby Christians, it's likely that many or most of them will stumble right out the back door.

If you are a parent, you know how exciting it is to see your baby take his or her first steps. Inevitably there are going to be some stumbles along the way, but first steps indicate that your child is maturing properly. One crucial step in learning to walk is the hand-holding stage, in which parents provide physical support and balance, protection from falls, and the encouragement that helps the child gain the skills and confidence needed to walk alone.

Some of you probably placed your trust in Jesus as a young child and may not remember what it was like to be a new believer. I was saved at age 17 while a senior in high school, so I vividly remember how much "hand-holding" I needed to begin my walk with Jesus. My spiritual legs were weak and wobbly, and I stumbled and fell more than I like to remember.

If you can think back to when you were a new Christian, which of these "helps" did you need to walk worthy of the Lord? *Mentally check all that apply.*

☐ Help in having the assurance that I was a child of God and was secure in His hands.

☐ Help learning why and how to pray.

☐ Help knowing how to deal with sins that kept occurring in my life.

☐ Help in learning how to read the Bible and where to start.

☐ Help in understanding the Bible well enough for it to make sense to me.

☐ Help in knowing how to tell people that Jesus had changed my life.

☐ Help in understanding why I needed to be in a good church—what a church could do for me and what and how I could contribute to my church.

☐ Help in understanding who the Holy Spirit is and what He does in and for me.

☐ Help in understanding baptism and why I should obey Jesus by being baptized.

I don't know about you, but I needed all of these—I REALLY did! And I suspect that the needs-list is pretty much the same for all of us. This would be especially true for those of us who, at best, may have been exposed to *churchianity* but never experienced true Christianity.

The theology of Good Soil Evangelism and Discipleship begins with the three accounts of the Parable of the Soils:

> 23 As for what was sown on good soil, this is the one who **hears the word and understands it***. He indeed bears fruit and yields, in one case a hundredfold, in another sixty, and in another thirty.
> Matthew 13:23
>
> ** Literally, "sees how it all fits together".*

> ²⁰ But those that were sown on the good soil are the ones who **hear the word and *accept it**** and bear fruit, thirtyfold and sixtyfold and a hundredfold.
> Mark 4:20
>
> ** Literally, "embrace it" or "welcome it with open arms".*

The first step to Christian discipleship is a genuine conversion—unbelievers must clearly understand the gospel, then sincerely embrace it.

If a person *clearly understands* the gospel of Jesus Christ and *genuinely embraces* Him as Savior, from the heart, we believe—based on Luke 8:15— this new believer will cling tightly to the word he or she has understood and embraced.

> ¹⁵ As for that in the good soil, they are those who, **hearing the word, *hold it fast*** in an honest and good heart, and bear fruit with patience.
> Luke 8:15

But just as we are to cooperate with God in evangelism—a divine-human process, God also uses more-mature believers to help baby Christians in their new life journey with Jesus. That's what we call "first-steps discipleship," and we see it in the New Testament.

For example, Paul and Peter encouraged their readers:

> ⁶ Therefore, as you received Christ Jesus the Lord, so walk in him, ⁷ rooted and built up in him and established in the faith, just as you were taught, abounding in thanksgiving.
> Colossians 2:6-7

> ² Like newborn infants, long for the pure spiritual milk, that by
> it you may grow up into salvation—
> ³ if indeed you have tasted that the Lord is good.
> 1 Peter 2:2-3

And Paul worked with them to stabilize them:

> ²⁴ Not that we lord it over your faith, but we work with you for
> your joy, for you stand firm in your faith.
> 2 Corinthians 1:24

What "First-Steps Discipleship" Means for YOU and YOUR Church

In a recent Barna Group survey, only 1% of church leaders said, "today's churches are doing 'very well' at discipling new and young believers." When looking at their own churches, 8% said they were doing "very well." It's just a guess on my part, but the 8% *might* be wishful thinking.

A TRULY evangelistic church, in the New Testament sense, will be concerned about more than evangelistic decisions—it will be equally passionate about and committed to nurturing new believers to experience a joyful and fruitful lifelong walk with Jesus.
Here's how that can happen in your church:

Congregational Discipleship: Your local church can and should be a "family" that warmly adopts new believers and lovingly nurtures them to maturity.

You have heard the old African proverb, "It takes a village to raise a child." Well, it takes a local church to raise a child of God effectively, but not just any kind of church.

As a 17-year-old baby believer, I began attending a small country church and joined a family of about 60 church members. They accepted me, loved me, taught me, helped train me; and sometimes they lovingly rebuked me when I needed it. I knew I belonged! I was fed spiritually from my pastor's sermons and Bible lessons and soon developed a desire to learn more about the Bible. *That little congregation discipled me!*

As I read the Book of Acts, it appears that most of what we now call discipleship was done in the context of church gatherings, especially in the earlier phases of the Church in Acts. No doubt the intimacy of assembling in house churches created a nurturing environment that was ideal for the assimilation and spiritual growth of new believers.

But church smallness doesn't *automatically* mean warmth and a welcome mat for new Christians. The median size of a church in the United States is about 70 members or less, with 40% of churches seeing 49 or fewer people attending their worship services. Most of these are small for a reason— they are declining congregations, declining because they have no vision, no outreach, and no motivation to improve or receive new members.

If you are a member or a pastor of a small congregation, you have a unique opportunity to build what, a few decades ago, was affectionately called "body life"—healthy New Testament congregational life. But you will have to make smallness work for you to achieve that, and sometimes that means reversing years of complacency.

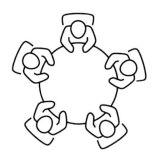

Group Discipleship: Assimilation into a Small Group can provide a nurturing family context.

I have never seen any statistics on this, but I'm guessing that it is more difficult for a new believer to survive and thrive in a large church than in a small congregation. As churches grow and become more institutionalized, the need for internal small groups increases. Properly organized and led, small groups can replace the loss of spiritual intimacy every believer needs somewhere in life, the family feeling of a house church.

To address the unique needs of new believers, some churches offer new convert classes periodically. That works best in congregations that are large enough to have enough young Christians to fill those classes on a regular basis. But when the class comes to an end, it is essential that these new Christians become assimilated into a fellowship where their journeys with Jesus can continue to be enriched.

Sensing the need to replace what gets lost in church growth, many medium-to-large size churches offer small groups. The foci of these churches vary, along with their names: Life Groups, Fellowship Groups, Cell Groups, Care Groups, Discipleship Groups, Bible Study Groups, and Home Bible Studies.

Unfortunately, these groups often become "closed groups," by design or by cliquishness—closed so tightly that new Christians cannot penetrate. And sometimes new believers join groups where the Christianese is so thick they can't decode the "foreign language." These kinds of small groups can do more harm than good.

Small groups require oversight to be sure they are staying on track, continuing to be warmly receptive and spiritually productive.

Personal Discipleship: Often, it's the *PERSONAL* touch that makes the deepest and most permanent impression.

Unfortunately, there are group discipleship devotees who pooh-pooh personal discipleship. Some will argue that discipling one person at a time is too slow and group discipleship is better because it produces more disciples in the same amount of time.

Your choice of discipling methodology shouldn't be based on devotion to one method or another but based on the 1.) needs of the potential disciple in the 2.) context of circumstances and the 3.) best way to meet those needs. When it comes to discipleship, quality is more important than quantity or speed. If the need is only for the acquisition of basic Bible knowledge, the development of spiritual disciplines, and fellowship, properly-focused small groups work well. But *mentoring*—the other side of discipleship—is best accomplished one-on-one.

I mentioned the discipleship I experienced by being in a small church "where everybody knew my name and they were always glad I came, where the troubles were all the same." No, it wasn't a bar—it was a Bible-believing country church.

But I didn't tell you about the deep and lasting impression my first pastor made on my life by *mentoring* me. Once he saw that I was committed to following Jesus, he met with me in his office and showed me which books would be most helpful to me as a young student of God's Word. He even drove me to the closest Christian bookstore, nearly 100 miles away, and helped me pick out a few basic Bible study resources. He opened the Bible with me and showed me how to "rightly handle the word of truth." He took me with him to make evangelistic visits with him, so that I could learn firsthand how to lead a person to faith in Jesus. When I began to preach, he sat down with me and explained how to outline a sermon, how to illustrate it, and gave me tips on how to present the message.

Mentoring—that's the other (and often neglected) important part of personal discipleship, and it can definitely best be done one-on-one.

If you were asked, "How well is your church doing in discipling new and young Christians?," on a scale of 1 (poor) to 10 (great) what would you say?

1   2   3   4   5   6   7   8   9   10

Here's a look forward to the remaining
"ESSENTIALS of a *Truly* Evangelistic Church":

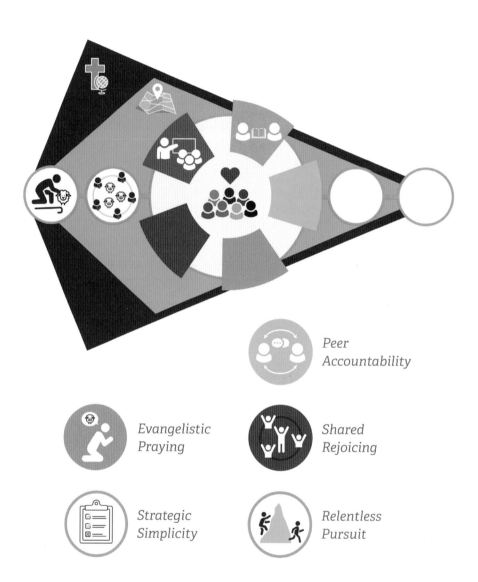

Peer
Accountability

Evangelistic
Praying

Shared
Rejoicing

Strategic
Simplicity

Relentless
Pursuit

Essential 7
Reflect & Act

Reflect:

1. What *helps* do you remember receiving as a new Christian? What kinds of *helps* do new Christians need?

2. Why is first-steps hand holding of new believers so important?

3. Explain the statement: "First-steps discipleship is a divine-human (combined) process."

4. What kind of church does it take to raise a child of God effectively?

Act:

1. If you had responded to the Barna Group survey, how would you have said your church is doing at discipling new and young believers?

2. Outline the ways, if any, that your church is accomplishing congregational, group, and personal discipleship.

3. Look for someone in your church who has never been involved in personal discipleship and might be open to you mentoring them.

Peer Accountability

*"One-Anothering" to Keep Believers
Mission-Focused*

Two-by-two, not one-by-one? *It took secular business corporations, medical professionals, and educators centuries to learn a principle that Jesus taught His followers 2,000 years ago.*

We all have important tasks that we (1) fear, or (2) dread, or (3) just don't prioritize as highly as we should. Consequently, we often fail to do them. For many of us who are Christians, witnessing to people whom we know need Jesus is probably on this list. That's why many, if not most, evangelical churches "talk the talk" of the Great Commission, but don't "walk the walk," at least on the local level. Good news: there is a game changer that is simple and effective.

What is the game changer? *It's the Peer Principle.*

We're all human, Christians or non-Christians. Often our churches can learn valuable lessons from research, organizational principles, and practices found to be productive by professionals in secular fields.

For example, medical teams have discovered that peer accountability is essential to insure that personnel are following appropriate safe practices. Businesses have learned that the most productive teams are those where peer-to-peer accountability is a part of the team culture. And there's plenty of research to support the value of the peer principle in a wide variety of contexts where people work together.

As students of the Bible, this should come as no surprise to us. Have you noticed the frequency of "one anothers" in the New Testament? There are 59 of them! While there isn't a "hold one another accountable to be a witness for Christ," admonition per se, some of the "one anothers" would encompass this essential Christian responsibility, especially these:

> Admonishing one another
> Colossians 3:16
>
> Encourage one another
> 1 Thessalonians 4:18; 5:11; Hebrews 3:13; 10:25
>
> Spur one another to love and good deeds
> Hebrews 10:24

The "one anothers" of Hebrews 10:24-25 appear in the context of assembling as a body of believers:

> [24] And let us consider how to stir up one another to love and good works, [25] not neglecting to meet together, as is the habit of some, but encouraging one another, and all the more as you see the Day drawing near.
> Hebrews 10:24-25 (ESV)

Fifty-nine (59!) "one anothers" in the New Testament—that's why Andy Stanley has said:

> *The primary activity of the church was one-anothering one another*
>
> *- Andy Stanley*

Implementing the Evangelistic Peer Principle in Your Church

Evangelism-focused "one-anothering one another" can be a game changer in the transformation of your church, from what it is to what you would like to see it become. Here's what you can do to make that happen in your church:

Evangelistic Peer Partners. Did you ever wonder why Jesus sent his disciples two-by-two on evangelistic campaigns? After all, two-by-two meant they were going to make half the number of contacts that could be made if each disciple went alone.

Think about it—why two-by-two? Based on some of my own experiences, I'm guessing it had a lot to do with mutual (peer) accountability, as well as support. It's definitely harder to "wimp out" when you are in the yoke with someone else. So why not transfer that wisdom of Jesus into your church's evangelistic ministry strategy?

All it takes to unleash the peer principle is two people in the church who are serious enough about the gospel that they are willing to enter into an evangelistic accountability relationship with each other. The goal: *stirring up one another* to love sinners and do the *good work* of sharing the life-changing good news about Jesus.

One set of evangelistic peer partners can set an example that will hopefully result in another set.

A Good-Shepherd pastor can spark this peer partnering by personal example—establishing the prototype partnership with another evangelism-minded man in the church. But here are some additional ideas for pastors to consider:

- Weave some of your evangelistic peer partnering experiences into sermons, where they are natural and most appropriate.

- Preach a series of messages on some of the key "one anothers" of the New Testament and tie some of those into the believer's responsibility to be actively engaged in personal evangelism.

- Throw out the challenge for other members of the congregation to find an evangelistic peer partner.
- Establish an official list of evangelistic peer partnerships and develop the concept into a simple and loosely structured church program, perhaps with a name more appealing than "evangelistic peer partnerships."

Evangelistic Peer Groups. Peer partners times two equals four, plus four more a little later equals eight, and on and on it grows. In this way, peer partnerships multiply into peer groups.

As committed Christians we know we have a responsibility to be witnesses for Jesus. He clearly commanded it. Furthermore, most of us feel constrained by love, compassion and conviction to see unbelievers saved, especially those we see regularly, such as neighbors or coworkers. Most of us need loving admonition (a Biblical word: νουθετέω/noutheteó!) to step out of our comfort zones and do what we know we should be doing. Admonition leads to action and positive action multiplies.

Evangelistic peer groups shouldn't replace peer partnerships, but there is something dynamically contagious about being part of a group where the focus is on rescuing lost souls from eternal damnation. Here are a couple of starter ideas for evangelistic peer groups:

- Start simple, with a monthly meeting where all of the evangelistic peer partners share their recent opportunities to "initiate conversations that may lead to redemptive relationships," "peel worldview onions," or  "bump people up the Good Soil E&D scale." This could be done in person or by means of an online meeting platform.
- Create a closed (by invitation only) social media group for sharing

evangelistic experiences or prayer requests.

Evangelistic Peer Congregation – the Ultimate Goal! It's exciting to see evangelistic accountability multiply within a congregation—a phenomenon known as "collective effervescence." When a group comes together to communicate a common vision and participate in activities to realize that vision, collective effervescence is created which excites individuals inside the group and attracts others to join the cause.

Meditate on this encouraging statement from Patrick Lencioni's business "The Table Group":

"If you and your teammates can master peer-to-peer accountability with each other, you have a game changer on your hands. Once you start to see and feel your productivity rising and the tension disappearing—you'll be humming."

Read the early chapters of Acts and you will see "Collective Evangelistic Effervescence" modeled for us.

Here's a look forward to the remaining
"ESSENTIALS of a *Truly* Evangelistic Church":

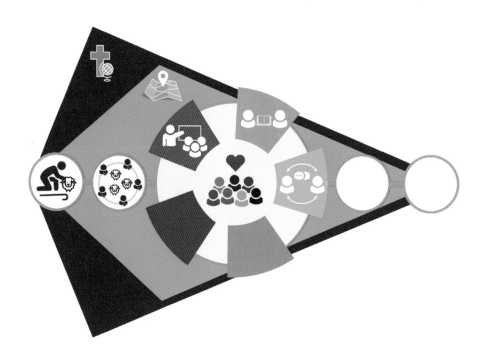

 Evangelistic Praying

 Shared Rejoicing

 Strategic Simplicity

 Relentless Pursuit

Essential 8
Reflect & Act

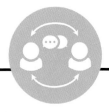

Reflect:

1. Do you think most people fail to evangelize out of fear, dread, or lack of prioritizing?

2. Why do many people balk at the idea of peer accountability?

3. What are some positive ways that peer accountability can be used in evangelism?

4. At the end of this chapter, it stated that the early church modeled "Collective Evangelistic Effervescence." What kind of local church image does this bring to mind?

Act:

1. Begin thinking and praying about who you might ask to be your evangelistic peer partner.

2. What do you think a pastor should be doing to encourage peer-partnering for evangelism?

3. Plan out what an evangelistic peer group would look like to you.

4. What step do you need to take next in response to this chapter?

5. What challenges might you encounter in implementing this essential in your church? How might you counter them?

Essential 9
Evangelistic Praying

*Prioritizing Congregational
Prayer Times*

Listen to the prayer requests in your church. They will tell you what your church folks value as they go before the throne of God. How many of the requests have eternity in view?

I suggest you try this a few times. Take note of the kinds of prayer requests your church members make. It's a great way to get a "feel" for the EQ (evangelistic quotient) of your congregation. Are they primarily "here and now" prayers, or "now and for all eternity prayers"?

The disciples of Jesus said, "Lord teach us to pray" in Luke 11. So our Lord gave them a model prayer, a prayer He didn't intend for them to recite verbatim. It was a prayer to teach them what kinds of things to pray about—priorities in praying. Yes, there should be priorities in praying.

It's certainly OK to pray for a loved one who is home with the flu or a friend who is having outpatient surgery tomorrow. There's nothing wrong with "here and now" prayers and prayer requests. All of us feel the need for prayer, as well as the urgency to pray for the temporal needs of others. So we want to be careful not to trivialize prayer requests that are sincere, even if they are not for extremely serious matters.

Evangelistic Praying

153

But most evangelical congregations need to be taught to prioritize their prayer times to focus more on lost sheep who need the Good Shepherd.

> [1] Finally, brothers, pray for us, that the word of the Lord may speed ahead and be honored, as happened among you...
> 2 Thessalonians 3:1
>
> [3] This is good, and it is pleasing in the sight of God our Savior, [4] who desires all people to be saved and to come to the knowledge of truth. [5] For there is one God, and there is one mediator between God and men, the man Christ Jesus, [6] who gave himself as a ransom for all, which is the testimony given at the proper time.
>
> [8] I desire then that in every place the men should pray...
> 1 Timothy 2:3-6, 8

Components of a Model Evangelistic Prayer Time

In a sense, our Lord has given us a model for evangelistic praying. Jesus started this model prayer Himself and finished it through the writings of the Apostle Paul. Pastors, you may want to teach your congregations this model:

One: Pray for Harvesters. My first mentoring pastor taught me that one of the best ways to get people to do something is by getting them to pray for that something to happen. For example, if you want them to get behind a building project, get them praying about the need for a building, etc. Prayer not only "moves God," it also moves the pray-ers to move with God.

> [37] Then he said to his disciples, "The harvest is plentiful, but the laborers are few; [38] therefore **pray earnestly to the *Lord of the harvest to send out laborers* into his harvest**."
> Matthew 9:37-38

Assuming His disciples prayed this prayer, they eventually learned that they were becoming partial answers to their own prayers.

Two: Pray for Opportunities. One reason Christians fear evangelism is because of the evangelistic method they have been taught, a push-the-door-open method, or even a knock-the-door-down approach. You probably know exactly what I mean.

When you go to someone's home, the visit will be much more pleasant and productive if they open the door and welcome you in, rather than forcing or inviting yourself in. Even Paul felt the need for open doors and believed that God (God!) could open doors for the gospel. And Paul believed that the prayers of other Christians were effective in helping make that happen.

> ³At the same time, **pray also for us, that God may open to us a door for the word**, to declare the mystery of Christ, on account of which I am in prison...
> Colossians 4:3

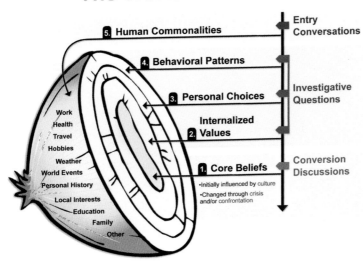

The Worldview Onion

In addition to a regular, perhaps daily, practice of praying for open doors for yourself and others, pray the "onion peeler's" prayer as you converse with unbelievers. The onion-peeling process, as taught by Good Soil Evangelism and Discipleship, is based on the open doors principle: Look for open doors for deeper levels of spiritual discussions with unbelievers. In the process of normal everyday *human commonality* conversations, pray silently for *entry points*—open doors that invite us to ask unoffensive investigative questions that may (or may not) lead to welcomed conversion discussions.

Three: Pray for Boldness. On a timid-to-bold scale, we might think that Paul was a "10." Well, maybe he was; but his boldness was empowered by more than personality.

> [18] praying at all times in the Spirit, with all prayer and supplication. To that end, keep alert with all perseverance, **making supplication for all the saints,**
> [19] **and also for me, that words may be given to me in opening my mouth *boldly* to proclaim the mystery of the gospel,** [20] for which I am an ambassador in chains, **that I may declare it *boldly*,** as I ought to speak.
> Ephesians 6:18-20

Paul's boldness was empowered by prayer—his prayers, no doubt, and the prayers of those who supported him—the same kind of power that his predecessor apostles experienced:

> [31] And **when they had prayed**, the place in which they were gathered together was shaken, and **they were all filled with the Holy Spirit and continued to speak the word of God with <u>boldness</u>.**
> Acts 4:31

Fear may be the number one reason Christians fail to witness for Jesus. Good preparation helps overcome fear, but prayer-based Holy Spirit empowerment energizes boldness.

Our fellow believers need to understand—it's OK to be fearful and it's OK to say, "Pray for me that God will give me the boldness to speak up for my Savior." Paul did.

Four: Pray for Clarity. Boldness in evangelism without clarity may be more harmful than no evangelism at all. Scores of people will probably spend eternity in hell because some bold Christian pressured them to say a prayer based on a "gospel pitch" that promised them heaven without clearly explaining the basis of saving faith.

According to Matthew, Jesus addressed the importance of clarity in messaging *the word* of God.

> [23] As for what was sown on good soil, this is the one who hears the word and **understands it**. He indeed bears fruit and yields, in one case a hundredfold, in another sixty, and in another thirty.
> Matthew 13:23

And even Paul, a seasoned veteran evangelist, requested prayer for clarity in his presentations of the gospel.

> [3] At the same time, **pray also for us**, that God may open to us a door for the word, to declare the mystery of Christ, on account of which I am in prison– [4] **that I may *make it clear***, which is how I ought to speak.
> Colossians 4:3-4

Clarity in content and clarity in presentation—these are the reasons we spend several hours in our Good Soil seminars focusing on how to help unbelievers clearly understand the gospel, even anti-believers with other deeply seated faith commitments.

Five: Pray for Receptive Hearts. As we have illustrated in the Good Soil Evangelism and Discipleship Scale, evangelism is a divine-human partnership. God has chosen to use us in presenting His message of redemption, but only He can convict, open hearts, and draw sinners to Himself. And, in some way that I do not totally understand, God responds to our prayers to convict sinners, open their hearts, and draw into His family the sinners we pray for.

Paul's "heart's desire and prayer to God" for Israel was "that they might be saved." (Romans 10:1)

And because this was Paul's heart's desire and personal prayer, he sought the supportive prayers of churches that wherever he went unbelievers would be receptive to his gospel ministry and message—Gentiles too, not just Israelites.

> [1] Finally, brothers, pray for us, **that the word of the Lord may speed ahead and be honored,** as happened among you...
> 2 Thessalonians 3:1

> [13] ...when you received the word of God, which you heard from us, **you accepted it not as the word of men but as what it really is, the word of God, which is at work in you believers.**
> 1 Thessalonians 2:13

If we really believe that God can convict sinners, open their hearts to the gospel, and draw them to Himself, why do we focus most of our prayers on earthly things that pale in comparison to the eternal destiny of our friends, family, neighbors—and the strangers God brings into our paths?

Leading Your Church in Evangelistic Praying

"Lord, teach us to pray." Followers of Jesus need to be taught how to pray and what to pray for. Our Lord is not among us in person, but He has left "under shepherds" (pastors) to carry out His will in the churches. For starters, here are some suggestions for leading a congregation in the ministry of evangelistic praying.

- Model evangelistic praying yourself. Let the congregation hear you practice what you teach.
- Don't allow all of the prayer time to be consumed with requests related to here and now needs. Divide the time into two periods, one for general requests, the other only for evangelistic requests—for harvesters, opportunities, boldness, clarity, and receptive hearts, etc.
- A significant part of peer accountability partnerships and groups should be their focus on prayer—prayer for specific unbelievers and gospel sharing opportunities, boldness, clarity, and receptivity.

- Teach the congregation the five types of evangelistic prayer requests mentioned above. A one-time ("one and done") sermon, or even one series of sermons, won't do it. Find some way to keep these emphasized in their minds.
- As part of these evangelistic seasons of prayer, allow for and encourage members to share answers to these prayers—what God is doing through their gospel ministries. It's the praise and thanksgiving part of evangelistic praying.

Here's a look forward to the remaining
"ESSENTIALS of a *Truly* Evangelistic Church":

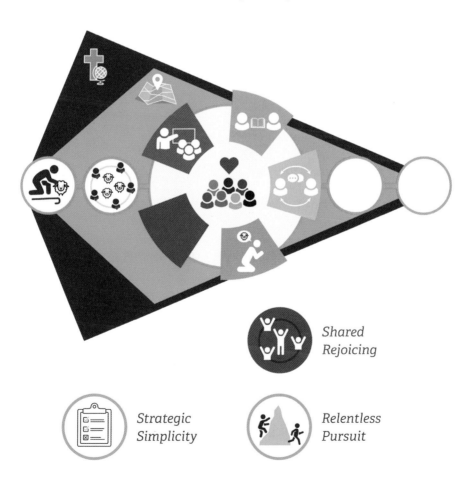

Shared Rejoicing

Strategic Simplicity

Relentless Pursuit

Essential 9

Reflect & Act

Reflect:

1. Study 1 Timothy 2:3-6. What is the real reason for Paul's desire for all to pray?

2. Why do you think many mission movements of the past began with a renewed concern of praying for the lost?

3. Why would the Apostle Paul need to ask for prayer for boldness and clarity in his evangelism?

4. Do you have confidence that prayer can open doors and change people's hearts?

Act:

1. How many of your prayers are focused on reaching "lost sheep"? What about those of your church?

2. Look back at your redemptive relationship list from page 94. Begin praying daily for them.

3. Consider some ways you might help your church to focus more on evangelistic prayers.

4. What step do you need to take next in response to this chapter?

5. What challenges might you encounter in implementing this essential in your church? How might you counter them?

Essential 10

Shared Rejoicing

*Celebrating What God and
His Angels Celebrate*

**We celebrate those things that bring us great joy—new babies,
graduations, weddings, birthdays, Super Bowl wins, and World Series
Championships. That's all good, but what do God and His angels celebrate
in heaven?**

Shouldn't our churches also celebrate what heaven is celebrating? And, if so,
what would that look like in your church?

Generally, Jesus told one parable to illustrate a truth He wanted people to
understand. But He told three parables in Luke 15 to explain heaven's value
of the human soul and the celebration that erupts in heaven when a sinner
repents. Obviously, Jesus wanted to make a point that His followers would
not miss. But have we missed it? Or have we just failed to fully grasp its
significance?

You probably know the stories of the lost and found sheep, the lost and
found coin, and the lost and found son. They are all woven around the same
themes: (1) something lost, (2) something found, (3) someone joyful.

But there's another theme you may have missed—the theme of (4) *Shared
Rejoicing.*

We will never feel the same degree of joy that our Holy God and his holy
angels experience when lost sinners repent and are adopted into the family
of God. As sinful, but forgiven, earthly creatures we are still too unholy for

⁶ "And when he comes home, **he calls together his friends and his neighbors, saying to them, 'Rejoice with me**, for I have found my sheep that was lost,'
⁷ Just so, I tell you, there will be more joy in heaven over one sinner who repents than over ninety-nine righteous persons who need no repentance."

⁹ "And when she has found it, **she calls together her friends and neighbors, saying, 'Rejoice with me**, for I have found the coin that I had lost.' ¹⁰ Just so, I tell you, there is joy before the angels of God over one sinner who repents."

²² "But the father said to his servants, 'Bring quickly the best robe, and put it on him, and put a ring on his hand, and shoes on his feet. ²³ And bring the fattened calf and kill it, and **let us eat and celebrate.**
²⁴ **For this my son was dead, and is alive again; he was lost, and is found.'** *And they began to celebrate.*"
Luke 15

that. But if there is little or no joy expressed in our congregations when people are saved, as church leaders we should be greatly concerned. And it is *our* responsibility to lead our congregations to share in the rejoicing with the new believer, his or her Christian loved ones, and those who were influential in leading him or her to the Savior.

There are two very special occasions in the gatherings of a local body of believers when heavenly rejoicing should resound in the church.

A Public Profession of Faith

According to Scripture, a verbal confession is the corollary action that follows a sinner's faith response from the heart. And every sincere profession of faith in Jesus Christ as Lord is cause for a celebration on earth, as well as in heaven.

> ⁹ because, if you confess with your mouth that Jesus is Lord and believe in your heart that God raised him from the dead, you will be saved. ¹⁰ For with the heart one believes and is justified, and with the mouth one confesses and is saved.
>
> Romans 10:9-10

When a man, woman, boy, or girl professes to trust Jesus as Savior and Lord, a vital part of the evangelism process is to inform the new believer of the need to tell others of his or her life-changing experience. The obvious first place for verbal confessions is among family members and friends. But it is also important that confession of personal faith in Jesus be made in a local congregation of believers, as the first step in identifying with a local church.

In an earlier chapter, I explained how the 60 or so members of the little country church where I was saved discipled me. That discipleship process began when they gathered around me and sincerely rejoiced with me after I professed my faith in Jesus—it was a celebration that I will never forget. It helped to bond me to those people who shared in my joy of salvation. And it began the process of congregational discipleship that was a vital part in setting me on a course to follow Jesus.

Congregations vary in how the celebration is done, but I suggest that this be done publicly in church, as soon as possible after the person is saved. And I also suggest that the person or people who played a role in this person's journey to faith stand with the new believer, as a sign of support and a demonstration of the fruits of personal evangelism. A public profession of faith should always be a time of celebration.

Joy is contagious! It contributes to the vitality of church life that Jesus intended for us to experience as we gather. And shared rejoicing motivates other believers to reach out to their unsaved friends.

A Baptismal Celebration

I wonder if the tone of a baptismal service is an indicator of how *truly* evangelistic a church is—how much the congregation values what God and

His angels value—how in tune the church is to the very reason Jesus came from heaven to earth. I'm just wondering. It's definitely something to think about.

I have observed baptismal services in many churches. In some churches people begin exiting the church as soon as the baptismal service begins. What kind of message does that send to the person identifying with Christ in baptism? In other churches, baptisms seem to be more of a dreaded *chore* than a blessed *celebration*. And in some churches the casual nature of this sacred event appears to have little more meaning than what happens with dunking machines at the church's annual picnic. I have observed them all! Perhaps you have also.

The baptism of a redeemed sinner should be the cause for a super celebration!

> *"Confession with the mouth is the evidence of the genuineness of faith."*
>
> - John Murray, 20th Century Scottish Theologian

I am happy to say that I have attended one church that really gets it. This church, a rather large church, schedules baptismal celebrations at certain times each year. Throughout the year, announcements are made explaining the importance and meaning of baptism, as well as the date of the next baptismal celebration.

The entire service is focused on baptism—what it means and what it doesn't mean. Candidates for baptism are asked to write their personal faith stories—how their lives have been changed by the gospel and who helped them along the way. Prior to the baptismal service, someone from the church helps to refine those stories and then they are recorded. As a candidate approaches the baptismal pool, his or her story is played for the congregation to hear. One or more key people who have been influential in the candidate's journey to faith in Christ accompany the candidate in the pool and even assist with the baptism. When the person being immersed is brought up out of the water, there is always spontaneous applause—a genuine sense of celebration!

I suggest that your church create its own unique plan for baptismal celebrations, with this as your guiding question:

What can our church do to reflect—as much as earthly possible— the mood that occurs in heaven when a sinner repents and identifies with Jesus Christ through believer's baptism?

In some ways, small congregations have more flexibility for baptismal celebrations. For example, you might take a hint from the prodigal son's father: "Let us **eat** and celebrate!"

Final Thoughts

In Good Soil Evangelism and Discipleship training seminars we say, "Regeneration is a point-in-time event, but conversion (in one sense of the term) is a gradual process." That is illustrated on the Good Soil Evangelism and Discipleship scale.

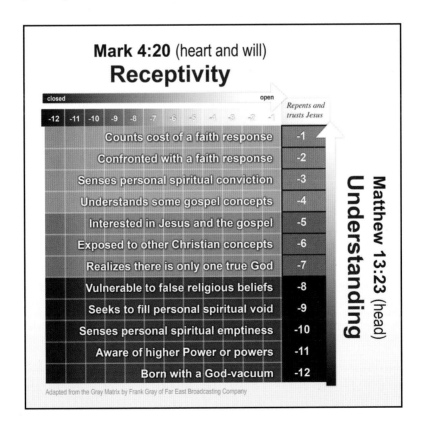

As is true with other unbelievers, prior to the morning I was born again, the Holy Spirit was working in my life—working to help me understand the gospel and softening my hard heart to be more receptive to the gospel. Understanding is the vertical dimension on the Good Soil E&D Scale and Receptivity is the horizontal dimension. God was moving me up the scale and across the scale.

Any time God uses us to "bump" an unbeliever up or across (to the right side of) the scale, that's something to rejoice in. Or any time a non-Christian friend responds positively to our witness, we feel the joy, so why not discreetly share that with other Christians who can experience our joy?

We know there is rejoicing in heaven when a sinner repents and when he or she publicly confesses "Jesus is my Savior and Lord" through believer's baptism. But surely there is also rejoicing in heaven every time a sinner's heart takes even the smallest turn toward God. Let's celebrate these positive responses to God and the gospel, as simple as they may seem at the time.

Here's a look forward to the remaining
"ESSENTIALS of a *Truly* Evangelistic Church":

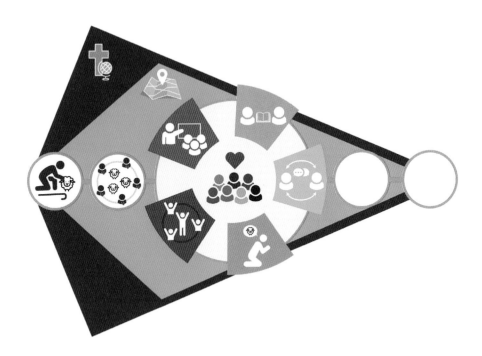

Strategic
Simplicity

Relentless
Pursuit

Essential 10
Reflect & Act

Reflect:

1. How significant is it that at the end of each parable in Luke 15 the finders say, "rejoice with me" and/or "let us celebrate?"

2. What do you think hinders us from expressing deep emotions, including deep joy, with other church members?

3. How excited do believers get about hearing of one who has made a faith response to the gospel?

4. What would make believer's baptism more joyful and meaningful?

Act:

1. What could your church do better to reflect the mood that happens in heaven when a sinner repents and turns to Christ?

2. Think of some scenarios where you can ask and give opportunities for people in your church to share their faith stories.

3. What step do you need to take next in response to this chapter?

4. What challenges might you encounter in implementing this essential in your church? How might you counter them?

Essential 11
Strategic Simplicity

Trimming What is Less Important
From Your Church's Activities

Many evangelical churches have added so many auxiliary programs and activities that they run out of steam before getting to the main things. What's the answer? Strategic simplicity!

Life in the New Testament church was simple—gather for fellowship, listen to the Scriptures expounded, pray, worship, praise the Savior who redeemed them, exhort one another to love and good works, and launch out to tell others about Jesus.

Five Realities Pastors and Churches Need to Face

First	Each of your church members has a limited amount of time and energy to spend in church-related activities.
Second	Church programming tends to grow from simplicity to complexity. Complexity is a subtle tendency; simplicity is a staunch choice.
Third	The more complex and diversified your church programming becomes, the more you must draw down on church members' time and energy to participate in and maintain those programs and, consequently, the quality and impact of ministry is diluted.
Fourth	Often, the problem of finding enough workers to staff ministry programs is not "too few workers" but "too many programs."
Fifth	Less important activities tend to replace the *essentials*, and evangelism is likely to be the first to go.

Through nearly 30 years of local church staff-level ministry in three very different churches, I learned that overprogramming can derail a church from genuine Great Commission priorities, but strategic simplicity can help maintain proper focus.

Good activities can become the enemy of the best: the essentials.

I have a small wooded area behind my house with many beautiful hardwood trees. But they are infested with huge boa constrictor-like vines that choke the trees to death. What's the solution? Cut the vines. The squirrels like the vines! The birds like the vines! In order to save the health of the trees I have to cut the vines, at least the ones that do the most damage.

Before you crank up the chainsaw, take care! People and programs are not vines. It is possible to cut too much and kill the trees. I've saved this ESSENTIAL for next to the last, not because it's not an essential ESSENTIAL, but because it's the most sensitive ESSENTIAL to tackle, especially for legacy churches that have been building programs for years.

Hopefully, after the congregation begins to see some evangelistic results and experiences some shared joy, church folks will better understand the need for strategic simplicity.

Five Simplifying Action Steps

Step One: **Clearly explain the strategy of simplicity.** Start with your leadership team, then plan a clear way to introduce your congregation to the idea. Perhaps a study on the New Testament church is a good way to start.

People transferring from other churches often want to bring the complexity of their former churches with them. I've heard more than a few of their, "We had this great program in our former church–I'd like to start it here" stories. The best way to deal with that is to clearly orient new members to your "strategic simplicity" approach to keep the church focusing on the essentials. Early on, they need to know and buy into the kind of church culture that exists—or that you hope will soon exist—in your church.

Step Two: **Don't start a new program or recurring activity unless it can pass the Great Co-missional litmus test.** Remember, a new program is much easier to start than it is to kill. The test: Does the suggested program *genuinely* and *significantly contribute* to the church's "Great Commission mission."

Step Three: **Review existing programs in light of New Testament essentials.** This is potentially a disruptive step—even a church splitter. Move carefully and slowly. Splitting the church is counterproductive to what you want to accomplish. In some cases, the following step (Step Four) can resolve the problem of programs that contribute little or nothing to THE mission.

But let me be clear, lest you misunderstand me: Obviously, evangelism is not the only essential in THE mission of the church. Worship, fellowship, Bible teaching, and compassion ministries are also essentials around which valid programs can, should, and must exist.

Step Four: **Where there is genuine and significant mission-potential, refine and refocus.** For example, churches often start church softball teams with the sincere goal of reaching men and women for Jesus and the church. But all too often, the goal of winning trophies eclipses the goal of developing redemptive relationships. It's a frequent case of mission drift. And sometimes bad behavior by some players on the team and fans in the stands becomes more of an evangelistic liability than a positive witness. If so, can your softball teams be redeemed and restored to productive outreach?

Another example: Most AWANA programs begin with the goal of reaching children, and parents, from non-Christian homes. Some churches experience amazing evangelistic success with AWANA and stay on track year after year.

But other churches lose sight of the original goal and AWANA devolves into a high maintenance, inward-focused, addition to Sunday school and children's church for church families. The church kids may love it and their parents probably appreciate the kids-care relief. But, in these cases, is AWANA accomplishing its most essential reasons for being? If not refocused, is it worth the time and energy drain on the church?

The difference is leadership—
persistently outreach-focused leadership.

Step Five: **Ultimately, if a program is not making a *genuine* AND *significant* contribution to an essential missional goal of the church, it should be eliminated.**

Genuine and *significant* are key words! Most anything done in the context of a local church can be justified as "ministry" by members who are strongly attached to the activity. But the question is:

Is this activity or program making a significant enough, genuine, results-producing contribution to our Lord's purpose for the church that it justifies the amount of time and energy (and, in some cases, money) expended to maintain and perpetuate it?

Or would the time and energy (and money) be best redirected to the more essential functions of your church?

While wisdom and tact are important in trimming the less-essentials, leaders often err on the side of being too cautious. Moving a church from complexity to simplicity will probably result in some collateral damage, maybe even the loss of some upset members. But if a few change-resistant insiders are preventing the church from reaching a neighborhood full of hell-bound outsiders, I think we know what a God-honoring, Christ-centered, Bible-believing local church should do.

Strategic Simplicity Works!

Many of the churches now making the most significant evangelistic impact are churches that have chosen strategic simplicity over strangling complexity. Andy Stanley, of North Point Community Church in Atlanta, stated North Point's rationale for simplicity in these words:

Ultimately what gets squeezed out of churches with complex programming is not ministry to believers but evangelism. Complexity kills the spirit of evangelism in the church because unchurched people never clamor for our attention. It's always the churched people who are asking for more programs. So eventually all the resources are consumed trying to keep insiders happy; meanwhile, the outsiders just go to the lake on Sunday morning.

In other words, complex programming is almost always inward-focused, leaving little or no congregational energy for reaching outsiders, the very ones who need the good news the Church has been commissioned to proclaim.

Final Thoughts

Writing this article has made me think about the "boa constrictor" vines that are choking the trees in my wooded lot to death. So I ordered a chainsaw to cut through the death grips of complexity. I'm going to be very careful as I cut the vines so as not to harm the trees and my little forest. But I don't want to be so careful that these choker-vines win. It's a tenuous balance, both for the trees and for our churches.

Metaphorically, this is the "moral of the story" of strategic simplicity in church ministry—cut the vines so the trees are healthier, but do it wisely so as not to kill the forest.

Of course, not all vines are destructive. Some vines are beautiful and fruitful. Jesus used a "good vine" cutting analogy in a parable about the vitality of believers' spiritual lives: Pruning, done right, is a key to fruitfulness! "Less" is the way to "more."

> [1] "I am the true vine, and my Father is the vinedresser.
> [2] Every branch in me that does not bear fruit he takes away, and every branch that does bear fruit he prunes, that it may bear more fruit."
> John 15:1-2 (ESV)

Here's a look forward to the remaining
"ESSENTIALS of a *Truly* Evangelistic Church":

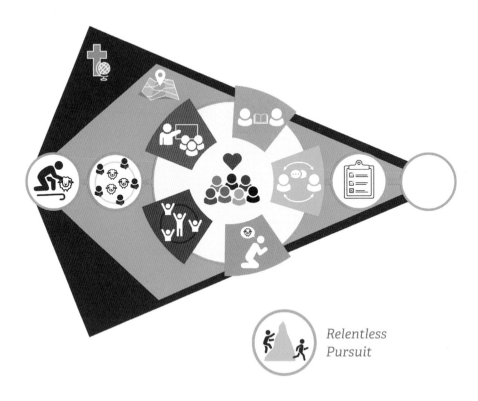

Relentless
Pursuit

Essential 11
Reflect & Act

Reflect:

1. Do you agree with the "Five Realities Churches Need to Face"? Do you think your church is aware of them?

2. How difficult is it to simplify the programming in a church?

3. Why would it be important to keep the concept of strategic simplicity before a congregation?

4. Why would it be important to introduce it to new members?

Act:

1. Which activities/programs do you deem may have strangled the essentials at your church?

2. Think through a best methodology (way to go about) cutting these kinds of programs at your church.

3. What step do you need to take next in response to this chapter?

4. What challenges might you encounter in implementing this essential in your church? How might you counter them?

Essential 12

Relentless Pursuit

Staying At It 'til Jesus Comes

The biggest challenge pastors face in leading a church in becoming TRULY evangelistic is not getting started, it's avoiding stopping. It's the DNF syndrome—"Did Not Finish"—that foils THE Mission.

"Spartan Race." It's an increasingly popular obstacle course race (OCR) based on the sport that was common in Ancient Greece, perhaps the kind of race the Apostle Paul had in mind when he used the race-metaphor in his epistles. All ministries have their obstacles, but because Satan has heaven-or-hell reasons to oppose evangelism, churches must be willing to relentlessly pursue the goal of rescuing sinners—under, over, and through some daunting obstacles.

The greatest challenge to implementing these "Essentials for a *truly* Evangelistic Church" may be the short-run syndrome—churches that start but stop when they encounter one or more of several obstacles. And there WILL be obstacles.

Two keys to overcoming them are (1) be aware of potential obstacles and (2) preplan, as much as possible, how to respond.

Common Obstacles to Long-Term Evangelistic Ministry

Opposition. Never in North American history has there been more external opposition to evangelism. Pluralism reigns, proclaiming: "All roads lead to heaven." "My religion is just as good as your religion." "How dare you say Jesus Christ is the ONLY way!"

And pluralism has even intimidated many Bible-believing Christians and churches. Terms like *saved, conversion,* and even *evangelism* are no longer in vogue in many so-called good churches. They have been replaced by a more politically correct and "less offensive" church vocabulary.

Many evangelical congregations haven't heard a Biblical sermon on hell in many years. Why? Because it's offensive—sometimes even to "evangelical" church members. Secular culture opposes the very essence of what the Bible teaches about lostness, eternal damnation, and the Bible's story of redemption. Leading your church to be Biblically countercultural with regard to proclaiming the gospel of Jesus Christ will be an uphill battle against the strong headwinds of liberalism, secularism, pluralism, multiculturalism, and agnosticism or atheism.

Then, there's the *internal opposition* from folks in your church who may value the status quo of a church that meets their needs and wants, more than they value seeing the gospel change the hearts, lives, and eternal destinies of hell-bound sinners.

Ultimately, to be truly evangelistic, a church must decide it's more important to focus on those they want to REACH as opposed to those they would like to KEEP.

Think: What would Jesus and the New Testament Apostles do if faced with those two options?

Distractions. "Missional Attention Deficit Disorder"—Yes, there's another kind of MADD and it's more common in churches than you may realize. Sometimes it occurs because the pastor is ADD (or ADHD). Seriously, there is something about pastoral ministry that seems to attract men with an Attention Deficit Disorder. A pastor with attention issues should seek professional help, else the church will struggle and fail.

Sometimes churches suffer from Missional Attention Deficit Disorder because they realize their ministry is failing but don't know what to do to fix it, so they blindly grasp for solutions.

And sometimes churches are MADD because they just seem to enjoy "chasing butterflies," always hopping on the latest ministry fad until another enticing one comes along.

The solution for Missional Attention Deficit Disorder:

First. Make the GREAT Commission, your church's TRUE mission—the "where you want to go." Decide what needs to be done to get there.

Second: Focus on the mission of making disciples, baptizing them, and teaching them to observe all things our Lord commanded. **And pursue it, relentlessly!**

The "Evangelism Essentials" in these chapters are **basic principles** necessary for churches to succeed Great Commissionally, **not a new "butterfly" program** to briefly chase then abandon. These principles are essential to getting a church back to a New Testament kind of lives-changing ministry.

Discouragement. The tortoise and hare have taught us well, but have we learned? It's not how you start; it's how you finish—a persistent pursuit of the goal is more important than a quick and flashy start.

"How quickly will these twelve principles begin to produce fruit in my church?" If you are looking for major quick-results, you probably will be discouraged. Resist discouragement by taking the long view and by enjoying small successes along the way.

There's a maxim in the commercial world—"Marketing won't bring results, but marketing plus patience will." You might want to convert that into a church ministry maxim and post it over your desk.

Fatigue. When I was a freshman student in a Christian college, the other students preparing for ministry let me know that there were two things I "needed" to do: (1) get "great preachers" to sign my Bible, and (2) choose a "life verse." Well, I never got into the great preacher thing, but having a life verse made sense to me. I didn't want to choose one of those common verses that a lot of other students had chosen, I wanted something unique. So I selected Galatians 6:9.

> [9] And let us not grow weary of doing good, for in due season we will reap, if we do not give up.
> Galatians 6:9 (ESV)

Little did I know, at that time, how much this verse would mean to me throughout the years of ministry that followed. I must confess that I have "grown weary" many, many times, but I have never "given up." Galatians 6:9 has kept me going. And it's a great theme verse to keep before the church in its "Spartan race" toward becoming *truly* evangelistic.

Pursuing lost sheep is a wearisome task. It is much easier for us to be inward-focused, inward with our fellowship of believers and inward with ourselves. But, for a committed disciple of Jesus, the question is NOT, "Is it easy?" But "Is it worth it?," and "Is it right?"

Pastoral Changes. Pastoral turnover can easily wipe out evangelistic momentum. Depending on whose survey you trust, the average tenure of a pastor at a local church is somewhere between five and seven years, although some surveys say less than five. Pastoral longevity or the lack thereof can be the make or break of a church.

Just imagine: suppose your church begins to make a serious effort to transform itself into a *truly* evangelistic body of Christ-followers and is experiencing some positive results. More than a few members are beginning to buy into the vision, the congregation is warming up, evangelistic prayers are becoming more frequent, and baptismal services are anticipated with excitement and experienced with shared joy. Then, the pastor who led in these efforts announces he is accepting a call to pastor another church. Ouch!

What are the chances your church will find another pastor who will pick up where the previous pastor left off? Odds are, he will come with his own agenda and priorities and most of what your congregation has gained will be lost.

For this reason, it is essential (there's that word again) that becoming a truly evangelistic church must become a local church-value, not just a pastor-value. As difficult as it may be, churches need to choose pastors who will meld with the church's values, rather than try to weld their own divergent ministry values on the congregation.

Final Thoughts

DNF = "Did Not Finish." There seems to be no public DNF statistics for Spartan races, but a common estimate is that less than half of the starters become finishers.

With some legitimate exceptions, DNF feels like a failure to serious runners—disappointing, embarrassing, even humiliating. In light of eternity, whether or not a runner finishes an earthly 5K race, marathon, or even a Spartan race is no big deal. But to be a DNF in races with the reward of incorruptible crowns, should and will be disappointing, embarrassing, and humiliating to Christians. The Apostle Paul pressed through many obstacles toward the goal that matters most.

> [13] ...But one thing I do: forgetting what lies behind and straining forward to what lies ahead, [14] I press on toward the goal for the prize of the upward call of God in Christ Jesus.
> Philippians 3:13-14 (ESV)
>
> [7] I have fought the good fight, I have finished the race, I have kept the faith.
> 2 Timothy 4:7 (ESV)

We want to help you and your church be a "finisher" in becoming *truly* evangelistic. That's why we extend an invitation to your church to become a part of the Echo Network: Helping Churches to Sound Forth the Gospel. The name "Echo" comes from a Greek word in 1 Thessalonians 1:8.

> [8] For not only has the word of the Lord sounded forth [literally, "echoed"] from you in Macedonia and Achaia, but your faith in God has gone forth everywhere, so that we need not say anything.
> 1 Thessalonians 1:8 (ESV)

As a member of the Echo Network, we will provide coaching for the pastor and other key church leaders, as well as regular opportunities for online networking sessions with other pastors.

For more information and to join the Echo Network, go to www.GoodSoil.com/Echo

Essential 12

Reflect & Act

Reflect:

1. What are the common obstacles to long-term evangelistic ministry?

2. Do you think our churches face more external or internal opposition to becoming truly evangelistic?

3. How do you react to this statement: "A church must decide it is more important to focus on those they want to **reach** as opposed to those they would like to **keep**.

4. Do you really want help to develop a long-term evangelistic ministry?

Act:

1. Develop some concrete steps to prepare for the obstacles you will face.

2. What might help you and your church avoid discouragement and fatigue?

3. Check out the possibility of your church joining the Echo Network.

4. What step do you need to take next in response to this chapter?

5. What challenges might you encounter in implementing this essential in your church? How might you counter them?

Conclusion

Experiences, frustrations, and conversations the authors have had through the years gave life to the narrative at the beginning of this book, although the characters you met in the story were fictional. But we can all identify with the challenges they faced. Perhaps you can identify with Brandon in particular. His heart was in the right place, but he was struggling to take the next step towards leading his church to become a truly evangelistic church. Brandon was blessed to have a circle of friends in whom he could confide, who guided him in the right direction. Over the following months and years, he was able to implement these twelve essentials to see great spiritual fruit in his church.

Wouldn't it be great to have a network of colleagues like Brandon had—a band of brothers who sharpen one another? Our Good Soil team would love to help. We have walked this journey and learned from our own mistakes. We also would like to help connect you to other church leaders who have a similar passion to reach their communities with the story of hope in Jesus Christ.

There are many ways you can begin this journey. You could...

- Come to one of our training events with two or three people from your church who will form your E-Team.
- Join the Echo Network and interact with other church leaders.
- Go through this book with your church's leadership, working through the Leader's Guide available as a free download from www.GoodSoil.com/TEC-LG.pdf

If you, like Brandon, would like to see your church become more active and effective in reaching people for Jesus, we can help by providing training, resources, coaching, and networking. If interested, call David Levy at (717) 909-2346 or write to info@GoodSoil.com.

Take that first step. Then be relentless in your pursuit of leading and being a TRULY evangelistic church.

ECHO
Network

Would you like to see your church become more active and effective in reaching unsaved people for Jesus?

We can help by providing:

- Training
- Resources

- Coaching
- Networking with Other Pastors

For more information visit: www.GoodSoil.com/Echo

Contact: info@GoodSoil.com • (717) 909-2346

Gaining Ground as a Truly Evangelistic Church

For not only has the word of the Lord sounded forth from you in Macedonia and Achaia, but your faith in God has gone forth everywhere...

1 Thessalonians 1:8